CASEY CHANEY

Author of "PARDON MY DUST...I'M REMODELING"

READY, WILLING & TERRIFIED

A Coward's Guide to Risk-Taking

ISBN 0-9626403-1-X
Library of Congress Catalog Card Number: 91-090118

First printing, May 1991

Cover design by Gary Craghead
&
Post Haste Publishing, Inc.

Mocha Publishing Company
8475 SW Morgan Drive
Beaverton, OR 97005

Printed in the United States of America

·   10 9 8 7 6 5 4 3 2 1

Dedication

To

Corey Michael Bruesch
Believe, my precious son, and follow your heart

and

Charles & Libby Chaney
You encouraged me to follow mine

and

Berdell Elizabeth Moffett
You taught me how

Acknowledgments

I would like to thank the following individuals for their outstanding work on this project:

Berdell Moffett: It has come to my conscious sagacity that I am exceedingly auspicious to have consolidated and centralized our acquaintance and occupational arrangement, and it would just tickle my fancy if you would stick around for a long, long time.

Vic Chaney: I know your *Projections* are right on, dear brother. Let's take them both to the top.

Meta Chaney: Amid the sounds of computer keys and printers comes the song of the Pink-beaked Burntwood Sister-In-Law Warbler— *Caannaaaaaastaaaaaa!!!!*—such a deal.

Thea Rhiannon: There are Editors, and then there are *Editors*, and then again, there are *EDITORS*. You, Thea, are an editor. I love you ~~alot allot alott~~ so much.

To Gary Craghead: Your graphic designing talents are well-coupled with your amazing intuitiveness. What a duo! May this be the beginning of a happy and prosperous career for you.

To Jay Fraser and Lynne Fulkerson from Post Haste, and to Paul Fitterer from Graphics 4: The only thing more outstanding than your typesetting and printing skills is your integrity. Thanks for a job well-timed and well done.

Special thanks to Denise Coy for the first reading and honest feedback; and to Diane, Richard, Iris, John, Sharon, Jan and Celia for your time, discerning eyeballs and great ideas.

and finally ...

Kila & Gonzo: I realize you two can't actually read this, but if only you knew the difference you make ... then again, you probably do ... and no, this does not mean you can get up on the couch!

Contents

PART THREE

Introduction

When the knowledge of the Power outweighs the fear of the condition, one can be healed.

—*Frederick Bailes*

Good news, folks! Risk-taking is really risk-*free*. There is actually no risk in taking risks. In fact, risk-taking is exciting, energizing, exhilarating, invigorating and just downright fun. And that's not all. As you take risks, you create your future. Taking risks makes you the architect of your own life. It sharpens your senses to amazing possibilities that ordinarily would have remained unnoticed.

Risk-taking is always, ALWAYS successful.

There is no such thing as a failed risk. The concept of failure is only an illusion created by the negative perception of a limited mind. Success, on the other hand, is created by a mind that thinks in terms of possibilities rather than impossibilities.

The consequence of a risk is not an end within itself. Seasoned riskers view each consequence as a new experience, an advanced education and one event in a stimulating progression of many events.

Life without risk-taking will eventually become boring. We can count on it. People terrified of taking risks usually extinguish their boredom by creating repetitive crises within their lives, rather than risk something new and experience the excitement of a new discovery. They create the same relationship problems, the same job dissatisfaction, the same loneliness and the same illness, over and over.

Reacting the same way again and again, even when it doesn't make life any better, appears to be more comfortable for some people than taking a risk. They fear that a new path will move them out of their so-called comfort zones. Comfort? Repeated anger and frustration is not comfortable. The truth is that they are only familiar, and that kind of familiarity you and I can do without.

The purpose of this book is to make *conscious* risk-taking a viable choice for you. To be conscious means that you are awake and aware of what you are doing. We all take risks on a daily basis; we are so accustomed to most of those risks that they actually go unnoticed. Conscious risk-taking means we are stepping into unfamiliar territory on purpose, with our eyes wide open in anticipation of change.

As I began to take risks, I noticed that there were patterns of responses from people, places and things around me that I could count on regardless of the kind of risk I was taking. This is what led me to the understanding that taking risks is indeed risk-free. I can predict certain reliable outcomes and work with those outcomes to the successful completion of my goals.

When I was just beginning to take risks, my biggest fear was of the unknown. I needed to have some sense that what I was risking was not going to leave me an emotional, physical and spiritual wreck. By getting in touch with the consistent responses from the universe after taking each risk, I have achieved my life's dreams at a remarkable speed. The result of my achievements is the foundation upon which this book has been written.

In all of my risk-taking, I have not lost a thing. My relationships with my family, my friends and my colleagues are prospering. I still have my cars, my home hasn't been repossessed, and my telephone still works. I hope that my next book will have the answer to permanent weight release (in other words, I'm not starving either).

You've picked up this book because the concept in the title relates to your life. Don't stop now. There is incredible joy in risk-taking. You can achieve more than you have ever imagined.

Casey Chaney
1991

Just What Is a Risk?

Wherever there is desire, coupled with a sense of apprehension or doubt, there is risk. A risk is anything that we think, say or do that has a questionable outcome.

Taking risks goes beyond the basic remodeling that I discussed in my first book, *Pardon My Dust ... I'm Remodeling*. In *Pardon My Dust ...*, the focus is to clean up what we already have. If our lives are uncomfortable in certain areas, we first find out what needs remodeling. Then we actively replace the old behaviors and attitudes using three simple guidelines.

Ready, Willing and Terrified is about becoming the architect of your own life; not just rebuilding what was uncomfortable, but creating a quality life beyond that. Stepping out means confronting the unfamiliar, and that means taking risks.

I decided to buy a home, realizing that the monthly financial output would be substantially higher than the rent I was paying. More furniture was needed, and I was now responsible for yard work. The attractive side to all of this was that I would have increased privacy, a nicer neighborhood and no more (ugh!) laundromats. It was something I really desired, but I questioned whether or not I could really manage it on a financial level. In other words, this was a risk.

We all take risks on a daily basis—little risks. Cooking something new, rearranging the furniture or changing a hairstyle are little risks. The bigger risks are the ones that threaten our feelings of safety. Starting a business, moving out of state or country, shooting the rapids or adopting an older child are bigger risks. When we awaken to the idea that there is more to life than familiarity, we become more willing to step into unfamiliar territory; and that means we take bigger risks.

All risks are calculated. We may not be familiar with the calculations, but nonetheless, they are calculated.

As you read along, you will begin to see how logical patterns of circumstances fall into place as risks are taken. You'll find yourself saying, "That's happened to me," because, whether you know it or not, you have already taken many bigger risks and experienced success with each of them. Now you're moving into the territory of conscious risk-taking. Are you ready? Willing? *Terrified?*

Ready and Willing

*B*efore any risk is consciously taken, there are two necessary ingredients: readiness and willingness. Readiness is a state of desire. "I'm ready for a new car," assumes that there is a desire for change. "I'm ready to parachute from an airplane," assumes that there is a longing to experience the thrill of jumping out of an airplane. Readiness is being open, emotionally, but that's as far as readiness goes.

Willingness adds dimension to readiness. When we are willing we are doing more than just being open to risk. With willingness there is also some action; a visit to the car dealership or signing up for parachuting lessons is action. Willingness is one step beyond readiness.

When we desire to achieve more in our lives, we become ready and willing to do whatever it takes. Then we are faced with following through on our little actions by stepping directly into the experience of risk-taking; actually buying the car or jumping from the airplane is the risk. Knowing what to expect from our risks helps us to eliminate the terrified. We become ready, willing and able.

Terrified

Terrified is another word for hesitancy, obsession, manipulation or unreasonableness—all various forms of terror and refusal to risk. We are terrified to take a step into the unknown. When there is terror, all the readiness and willingness in the world is useless.

Terror isn't usually logical. It is caused, for the most part, by focusing on the worst possible result of a risk. Until the worst scenario actually happens, it isn't real. Most riskers find that the worst possible scenario never happens. So, what we are afraid of is a house of horrors born of our own negative imaginations. The result of our terror is that we continue to live with unfulfilled dreams.

One of my dreams was to find my right livelihood. I was very ready for the change. I was even willing to take less money for my services. But I feared doing the one thing that I needed to do to create unlimited possibilities for me: I feared quitting the job I had in order to find the one I wanted. My particular teaching position required so much of my time and energy that I couldn't focus on finding a new career. There were no half-time positions available, so the only alternative was to quit teaching completely.

The excuses and rationalizations I used were all based on my fears of the unknown. Since my spouse and I were having severe difficulties and didn't know if we were going to stay together, I worried about my basic survival. What if I couldn't find a job at all? What if I couldn't pay my mortgage? What if I lost my house? What if I couldn't feed my child?

Though my fears appeared to be well-founded and rational, they had me paralyzed. I continued for years to live the kind of life I didn't want because I refused to take the necessary risks.

Can you relate to this? Do you have any unfulfilled dreams? Are you intimidated and/or deterred from your dreams by your fears?

Intimidated

The word *intimidate* means to scare through the use of threats. We should do this, we'd better do that, or else. ... or else *what?* This is where the majority of us get stuck. When asked, "...or else *what?*" by someone many years ago, I replied, "... or else I'll be out of money and I won't be able to pay my house payment or my bills."

"So?" replied my confrontational friend.

"So ... I'll lose my house!" I retorted in exasperation. "My son and I will be out on the streets!"

"Will you *really?*" she asked with a lilt in her voice that smacked of an "Oh, come now" attitude.

"Yes, we will!" I shouted emphatically. (I was sure I had won this argument.)

"Congratulations ... you win," she replied, reading my mind. "I didn't realize you were so incapable that you couldn't come up with a better alternative than living on the streets."

The truth in this case was that I was intimidated by my own "impossibility thinking." Upon further evaluation of my circumstances, thinking through and beyond all of the worst case scenarios, I realized my friend was right. There were other possibilities.

Many times we are ready and willing to take a risk when, suddenly, we are confronted by someone engulfed in his or her own form of impossibility thinking. That person begins to reflect back to us our own fears. Often, such people are our close friends, associates and particularly our families.

My family members reflect my fears because they love me and worry about me. When I risk doing something out of the ordinary (like deciding to write self-help books for a living) they say things like, "How are you going to pay your house payments and your bills? You'll be living out on the streets if you're not careful! Remember you have a little boy to take care of!" It never ceases to amaze me how accurately my loved ones can express my own thoughts of impossibility.

Usually, people do not intend to intimidate us; and even if it is their intention, they don't actually do the intimidating. They simply illuminate the very fearful and limited thoughts we harbor deep in the recesses of our own minds. The result is that we *feel* intimidated; we *feel* impossible and hopeless.

In the process of reacting to impossibility thinking, we mentally and emotionally suffocate ourselves. Statements such as "I can't ..." and "It won't work ..." and "There's no way ..." are made on the assumption of logic. Though it may appear that impossibility thinking is realistic or logical thinking, it is really nothing other than a negative attitude.

At one time, it was considered unrealistic to expect human-kind to fly. It was illogical to think a positive attitude could cure heart disease or cancer. Not any longer. Why? Because people who were willing to risk ridicule set out to prove that there was another reality; and they did it. Common sense was replaced by uncommon sense, and it worked even better.

For as long as we remain intimidated, buying into fearful, limiting thoughts and illusions, we remain terrified. When we are ready and willing to move beyond impossibility thinking, intimidation dissipates, and we move one step further from terrified and one step closer to able.

Deterred

The word *deterred* means to be detained or detoured from taking action. Isn't that exactly what happens to us? We end up postponing what we really want in our lives, or we run off on wild goose chases because we are deterred by our impossibility thinking.

Detained

We allow ourselves to be detained in order to avoid feeling terrified. We do this by attempting to tie up all of the loose ends before we take action. Of course, this appears to be the realistic and logical way to do things, but the universe refuses to stand still. What may appear to be tied together can be untied in an instant, leaving another end dangling free.

I wanted to move back to Oregon in 1981. Rather than give notice to my job and put my house up for sale at that time, I decided to "tie up the loose ends" first. Some of the loose ends included getting my Oregon teaching certificate and securing a job there before moving. This was the realistic and logical thing to do. One by one, as I tied up the loose ends, more loose ends took their places.

Three years later, I still hadn't moved. Finally, I gave up trying to tie up the loose ends and prepared myself to move even without the security of my teaching certificate or an awaiting income. My financial situation was actually worse than it had been three years before. Regardless, I was ready to walk away from the dubious comfort of familiarity and willing to risk the unknown. As it turned out, I made my move and secured a teaching job in two days, even without certification.

Detoured

Another way we avoid feeling terrified is to take a detour. We think we're taking the shortest route because it's more familiar or it makes more common sense. This constitutes the appearance of logic in our minds. Unfortunately, though this common sense may seem logical, it isn't always the case.

Take, for example, the story of the Panama Canal. Before it was the Panama Canal, ships had to sail around the entire continent of South America to get from the Atlantic Ocean to the Pacific Ocean. This meant an 8,000-mile detour.

The French were the first to attempt to dig through the 40 mile strip of land in Panama. After 20,000 people working on the Canal died from Yellow Fever, the entire project was called off. When it was finally learned that mosquitos were the carriers of the disease, the French became paralyzed with impossibility thinking. They resigned themselves to sailing 8,000 miles around Cape Horn rather than risk tackling the mosquitos. Because of their fear of Yellow Fever, it seemed more logical to take the longer route. Fortunately, there was a better answer.

Teddy Roosevelt was a possibility thinker. As President of the

United States at the time, he decided to launch a major cleanup of the area that included spraying insecticides and building roads to eliminate the muddy breeding grounds of the mosquitos. It was a big risk that many people criticized—until they saw that it worked.

We frequently react as the French did. Rather than dig a canal, we take a slow boat around the Cape. After all, we already know what it feels like to be seasick and suffer the consequences of a sinking ship. Why risk the possibility of mosquitos and Yellow Fever? So instead of taking a risk to find a solution, we choose the longer, more familiar route. The result is that we use an outlandish amount of negative time and energy to achieve one goal. Setting and achieving our goals becomes exhausting and disappointing.

With so little accomplished as the result of our detentions and detours, our dreams and desires become painful thoughts of failure and hopelessness. We stop dreaming, and we choose instead to accept a life of boredom and repetitive crises.

Being terrified, then, means that we are intimidated (detained or detoured) from taking risks due to our limited, impossibility thinking. We put a negative caption on an incomplete picture and leave the picture unfinished. The unknown is so intimidating that we become intentionally stuck in the muck and mire of our lives. So, how do we overcome the terror? We define the unknown by facing it—squarely.

The Unknown

The one blank page you have just experienced was placed there intentionally to illustrate a point. Blank pages where there aren't supposed to be blank pages make us uncomfortable. We begin to wonder if something is wrong or missing. "What was supposed to be there?" we may ask. The answer is that nothing was supposed to be there. When a page is blank, we are presented with unlimited opportunities.

A blank page (aka the unknown) is the basis for all creativity. It is here that we have the opportunities to use our imaginations to their fullest. For this reason, it is necessary to practice positive possibility thinking. We want to compose and initiate a healthy, happy and prosperous future.

When we are filled with thoughts of impossibility, we fill our blank pages with pictures of worst case scenarios. This in turn creates our emotional paralysis. Why bother attempting the impossible? We have actually assumed the worst and created a gloomy and unfavorable concept of reality.

Even if our pessimistic images are based on a real past experience, we can be sure that the experience was poor because of our chronic pessimism. We were as much impossibility thinkers then as now. What appeared as "bad" had some solid elements of "good," but we weren't willing to see the situation from another viewpoint. We were simply shut down to the opportunities that were available.

Opportunities Or Setbacks?

You may notice that I use the term *appearance* quite often. This is because appearances are not necessarily reality. An appearance is a judgment we make based on the perception we have of a situation. If we perceive the situation from a negative viewpoint, then the situation appears negative; from a positive viewpoint, the situation appears positive.

A good friend of mine called me up one day, despondent and terrified. She was given notice at her job due to some layoffs. Realizing she was fearful of the unknown, I said, "Congratulations!" She was perplexed by my seeming lack of understanding. Here she was, in pain and terror, calling me for sympathy, and I responded by being facetious.

But I was not being facetious at all. I was *living* serious (as opposed to *dead* serious—see the positive perspective?) Coming from a positive perspective, I know that when one door closes, a better one opens. Though she was still somewhat terrified, she began to see her lay-off as an opportunity rather than a setback. Within one month, she had established her own business doing what she loved to do. Since then she has been featured in the newspaper, and she maintains a growing clientele.

Without her readiness and willingness to risk a different attitude, she would not have risked starting her own business. She would probably have sought out another position similar to the one from which she was laid off. This might have meant choosing another lay-off as well. Future unknowns would most likely be handled with the same fearful, negative vision, and ultimately, the same negative decisions and consequences. The same miserable cycle would continue with different names and faces. Wherever we go, there we are.

How often have you run into the same negative conditions without changing your perception of them? This could include repetitive arguments with certain people or finding yourself in re-occurring traffic jams.

Whatever the adverse condition, you are essentially writing and rewriting the blank page of the unknown with your impossibility thinking. When you use possibility thinking, those adverse conditions transform themselves into harmonious conditions.

Your blank page is your coloring book. Illustrate it imaginatively using colorful and exciting possibilities. In other words, define your unknown with optimism.

If you are anything like me, right about now you will probably be saying to yourself, "How do I define my unknown with optimism when I'm still terrified?" The answer to this is simple: When you understand how to predict certain outcomes and how to work with them toward achieving success, your terror is greatly minimized.

The following section is designed to do just that. It is the process for identifying the outcomes of your risks and knowing what steps to take along the way.

P A R T   T W O

The Ultimate Partnership

*T*here is a Partnership between you and the universe. It's very simple. You risk, and the universe responds. The universe responds harmoniously to all of the risks you take. I refer to this consistent risk/response concept as The Ultimate Partnership. Getting to know and understand the way this Partnership works eliminates the terror of taking risks.

There are Seven Basic Risks that we take in building our lives more fully. With each of them, we experience a specific response from the universe. Here are the Seven Basic Risks and Universal Responses of this Partnership:

	Risk		Universal Response
#1	Believing	➡	Vision
#2	Choosing	➡	Direction
#3	Action	➡	Details
#4	Integrity	➡	Miracles
#5	Acknowledgment	➡	Students
#6	Teaching	➡	Recess
#7	Contemplating & Meditating	➡	Greater Visions

RISK #1

The Risk To Believe

	Risk	Universal Response
#1	Believing	

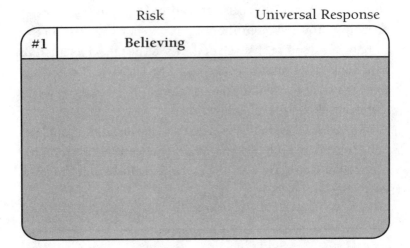

T he first risk is to believe in possibility. This is the most important risk any of us will take in a lifetime. The person who believes, achieves. When the sense of possibility is greater than the sense of impossibility, the scales are tipped for success. We have been told by every spiritual leader from Abraham to Buddha that it takes only a miniscule amount of believing to tip those scales in our favor.

Believing is the first step toward custom-building our lives. Compare this to living in a model home or building a dream home. We have essentially been living in "model lives," accepting what other "builders" have claimed was possible for us. We could see no other options.

As we risk believing in possibility, we become the architects of our lives. By putting that belief into action, we become the builders. Committing to believe means putting that belief into our thoughts, words and behaviors, unconditionally. When we do this, our lives take on a custom-built look, and that is a look of quality.

Think about a time in your life when you achieved some dream, desire or idea. There was probably a sense within you that attainment was possible. Your belief in possibility was greater than your belief in impossibility, or your vision would not— could not—have manifested.

I wanted a piano for quite some time. There was no apparent means to the fulfillment of this desire, but I knew that at some point I would have a piano. One day, a new friend came to my home for lunch. Knowing that I was a musician, she was astonished that I did not own a piano. She promptly decided to give me hers. Her grandmother had given it to her years before, and it had remained unplayed all during that time. Not any more.

When I decided to write my first book I knew without a doubt that it would be published. I believed; and what appeared to many of those around me as impossible soon became a reality. It all began with my sense of certainty, my believing.

Hoping vs. Believing

Believing is risky because we tend to mix up the idea of believing with the idea of hoping. The two are completely different concepts. Even though hoping implies a positive attitude, there is still an element of uncertainty. We hope against hope.

When we believe, there is no room in our consciousness for uncertainty or skepticism. We simply know within ourselves that we will achieve the goal. We believe because we have decided. Our minds are made up that we will achieve, and nothing is more powerful than the made-up mind. The made-up mind does not hope; it believes.

Believing In The Power

Believing that we are in a Partnership with some unseen Power is a necessary ingredient to understanding and using this process. How you think of this Power is a matter of personal choice. Think of this Power as God or undiscovered laws of physics or Mother Nature or Higher Power or anything else that is comfortable for you. I use the term *universe* to symbolize the unlimited nature of the Power.

Sometimes we make a half-hearted attempt at believing and end up with few or no results, claiming, "See! I tried believing, and nothing much happened." Half-hearted attempts at believing are characterized by waiting for the Power to prove itself. Then when the world fails to look the way we think it ought to, we claim we have proof that the Power doesn't exist.

I was ranked among the more stubborn and obstinate of those who had difficulty coming to the decision to believe. I used to think that, if there was a Power, it was some kind of personality that was hiding and would show itself if it was real. It never occurred to me that this Power was similar to the power of electricity; that certain elements, brought together, released its potential. Those elements are the Seven Basic Risks, *believing* being the first.

I came to believe when nothing else seemed to be working to ease the pain and dissatisfaction in my life. My marriage was constantly in turmoil, I was unbearably stressed out over pressures at work, and I seemed to have no friends. I thought to myself, "Why not put your pride on hold for a while and open up to the possibility? After all, there just might be something to this." Then I started digging for answers.

I began by exploring and contemplating all of the coincidences in my life. A small but profound example of this occurred when I took my son for a haircut after school one day. I had planned to make an important shopping trip after he was finished and before going home. This would have taken about 45 minutes. For some reason it didn't feel right to do the shopping and I decided to go on home instead.

As we were pulling into our driveway, my son exclaimed, "Oh, I forgot! I have basketball practice today, and I have to be there at 5:00 p.m. sharp or I won't be able to play in our first game." It was 4:45 p.m. He had just enough time to dress down for practice and get over to the school. Had I gone shopping, we would have been too late.

What was it that entered my mind at just the right moment to guide me home instead of to the store? This kind of "coincidence" had happened so many times that I finally began to wonder if there was indeed some incredible Power guiding me, even when I didn't know I was being guided. I certainly didn't feel any different while it was happening. It was after the incident that I would realize something remarkable had just taken place.

21

I could have continued to call it luck, or I could admit that I had just consciously discovered a Power. At the point in my life when I was experiencing the most difficulty, I chose to believe it was a Power.

The Made-Up Mind

When we make up our minds that something is going to happen, believing takes place automatically, and our goals are achieved. I believed that my piano would appear one day, and I believed that my first book would be published. My mind was made up about these things.

Our decisions and behaviors will substantiate our beliefs. If we say that we believe in a certain political stance and then vote opposite to that stance, what does that say about our true belief? If we say that we believe honesty is the best policy, and then we lie, cheat or steal, what does that say about our true belief? If we say that we believe flying is safe, and then we refuse to get on a jet, what does that say about our true belief? Few of us want to exercise hypocrisy. The made-up mind is a no-matter-what proposition. It overcomes all appearances of obstacles.

Creating The Made-Up Mind

One way to create a definitive, decisive attitude toward a goal is to explore your own past experiences. Think of a time when you made a decision with no hesitancy, even when there were elements that could have been construed as obstacles, and you still succeeded in attaining your goal.

What did that feel like? Exercise inserting that sensation into an area where you are struggling to believe. Practice. You may not experience a lasting feeling of belief right away, but with practice it gets better.

Seek out people who are accomplished believers. By accomplished I mean people whose lives reflect the attainment of their dreams, desires and ideas. This does not mean they have picture-perfect lives; they experience setbacks and challenges as well. It means they are achieving regularly scheduled goals. Listen to them. They know what they are talking about, and they are incredibly inspiring. They will help you to believe because they believe for you as well as for themselves. They know that whatever is possible for one is possible for all. Until we have learned to believe and achieve consistently, we don't always understand this very important fact.

Our disenchantment and doubt is so quick to tangle us up emotionally that we cannot always see the positive perspective. Listening to others who are possibility thinkers, pulls us out of our muddy vision and into focus once again. We are virtually lifted, and our emotional load is lightened.

Avoid discussing your aspirations with those who are doomsayers unless you have achieved a state of believing that is unshakable. As soon as you realize a person is caught up in impossibility thinking, make an effort to close or change the conversation. You want inspiration, not expiration.

If you find you have reacted negatively or fearfully to another's doubting attitude, simply notice yourself reacting. Say to yourself, "Aha, I see all that doubt and insecurity deep down there." Exposing that fear takes the wind out of its sails.

When we finally begin the process of conscious believing, the universe begins to respond. The Ultimate Partnership is initiated by our first risk—believing.

RESPONSE #1

Vision

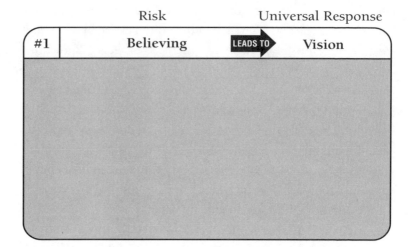

#1	Risk		Universal Response
	Believing	**LEADS TO**	Vision

The universe responds to our risk of believing by sending us a clear vision for our lives. Before believing, our dreams seemed like pleasurable thoughts for a distant or unlikely future. We allowed them to float around our heads like nebulous clouds. They were fuzzy and only remotely recognizable.

Through believing, we watch, we listen, we become attentive. Once we begin to believe in unlimited possibilities, even just a little, the real visions for our lives suddenly take on clarity. Our true hopes and dreams become exposed to our conscious awareness. They take on the aura of concrete objectives. They now have the essence of substance.

Have you ever been unclear about what you really wanted out of life? Try taking the risk of believing in unlimited possibility, and you'll suddenly find yourself with a powerful vision for your life. The universe will send an influx of clear vision to flood your mind, and you'll feel the joy that accompanies it.

When I applied for a teaching position many years ago, the interviewing principal asked me where I saw myself in five years. I laughed. I couldn't even picture myself within one year, let alone five years. I was a disbeliever. I saw limitations instead of possibilities, and the result was a huge blind spot. I saw nothing, and I had been living in this state of nothingness for years.

Murky-mindedness is the result of disbelief. When we don't believe in possibility, we tend to cover our dreams, desires and ideas with a mental shroud. The vision we have for ourselves is there; it's just camouflaged with disbelief. When we believe in unlimited possibilities, our vision is clear.

Often, we think we have a vision when what we really have is a "supposed to." "I'm supposed to be a housewife like my mother." "I'm supposed to stay at the same job for 35 years and retire with a gold watch." Some people use "should" instead of "supposed to." "I should have a big house." "I should have a dog." "I should be married." These so-called visions are not visions if they do not represent what you really want. They are more like living nightmares. These "shoulds" and "supposed tos" are the results of the limited thinking induced by a disbelieving mind.

Believing helps us to be mentally present to receive our true vision. This is very important, because it is the vision that encompasses the directions for a life filled with health, prosperity and happiness.

RISK #2

The Risk To Choose

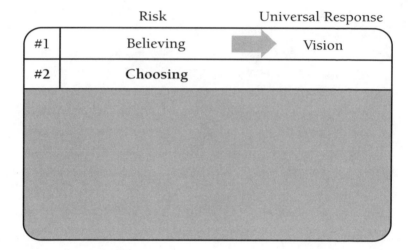

	Risk	Universal Response
#1	Believing	Vision
#2	Choosing	

When our dreams, desires and ideas become clear to us, we are actually being presented with our choices. This is when we identify what we really want in our lives. As we specify what we really want, we experience excitement about its possibilities. It becomes painful even to think about accepting less.

This is why choosing is risky. We avoid getting specific about what we want in order to avoid disappointment. We have terror around the idea that we might deeply desire something and not get it. But this sensation of desire is what initiates the next response from the universe. Without it, the vision will not materialize. So, choose we must.

At this stage, we are concerned only with *what* we are desiring, not with *how* we are going to achieve it. The *how* is none of our business; the universe will work out those considerations as we take the Seven Risks.

Choosing The Honest Dream

Choosing requires us to get honest with ourselves. If you think to yourself, "I really want this, but I know it won't be possible so I'll take that instead," you are being dishonest with the universe and the Ultimate Partnership comes to an impasse. The reason for this is that the Partnership depends upon your willingness to believe. By doubting the possibility of having your true vision manifested, you are taking a step backward. If you resign yourself to accepting less than you really want, it's because you lack belief. That's why so many of us are still left with unfulfilled dreams—me included.

We have a habit of trying to figure out the *hows* before we get absolutely honest about what we really want. We then make choices based on what we think we can achieve rather than on what we really want. Since the Ultimate Partnership relies upon honesty in order to fully disburse its Power, any dishonesty creates delays in our achievements.

Six years ago, my honest dream was to be a writer, speaker and workshop facilitator. Thinking this dream was impossible at the time, I quit teaching and began a typesetting business out of my home. I thought this would sustain me and still give me the time to write. As it turned out, it only sustained me when I worked overtime and on weekends, and then I was too harried to write anything.

I ended up taking out several large loans to finance my business. Looking back, I would have been better off financially if I had begun writing full time and used a loan to help me through my transition from teaching to authoring books. This would have been my honest dream. Instead, I took action toward a dishonest dream—one that I thought I could achieve, but that I did not prefer. It wasn't that I hated what I was doing. It's just that I would have preferred doing something else. The result was years of subtle job dissatisfaction.

We must learn to choose the honest dream, no matter how impossible it may appear, and let the Power of the Ultimate Partnership move us toward its manifestation.

Prioritizing Our Dreams

Prioritizing is an area in which many people get stuck. They have come to believe in the exciting possibility of having the life they want. Suddenly, all of these long-forgotten dreams and visions come galloping out of the deep recesses of their memories, only to create mass confusion. "Which dream should I concentrate on getting first?" is a common question asked of me.

First of all, more than one dream can be manifested at a time. Our priorities change daily. This is a natural part of the scheme of life. Little by little we find ourselves taking steps toward all of them, depending upon the priority of the day. If you are confused or overwhelmed on a certain day, there are a number of alternatives.

One way is to list, on a piece of paper, all of your dreams or visions, then cut each one out individually. Now, make a game of it. Pretend you have to give up one of those dreams. Throw it away. Do the same thing over and over with the rest of them until you are left with only one. It's okay to rearrange them at any time. This is just for the purpose of focusing and prioritizing.

Another way to prioritize is to ask yourself where your negative energy is. Negative energy is the feeling of desperation that often goes along with wanting to achieve a goal. It could be characterized by guilt, doubt, fear, shame, resentment, and so on. This negative energy creates disbelief. The solution out of this dilemma is to find the goals with the least amount of negative energy, and take steps to achieve them first.

To begin this way of prioritizing, make a list of all the things you feel the most desperate about achieving. Start by filling in the blank with the most desperate goal: "If only (fill in what you want to achieve), my life would be great." Then pretend that this dream has already been fulfilled. Now do the same thing again using another of your unfulfilled visions. And again ... and again ... When you are finished, you will have a list of unfulfilled dreams that are obstructed by negative energy. The one on top carries the most. The one on the bottom, the least. Here's an example of how I create my list:

1) If only I was 50 lbs. lighter, my life would be great.
   (Suppose this has been accomplished. Now what is lacking in my life? List the next goal.)
2) If only I had more money, my life would be great.

(Suppose this has been accomplished. Now what is lacking in my life? List the next goal.)

3) If only my house was more organized, my life would be great. (Suppose this has been accomplished. Now what is lacking in my life? List the next goal.)

4) If only my garage was cleaned out, my life would be great.

Now I have four visions that contain negative energy, beginning with the one that seems to carry the most today:

1) I want to attain my perfect body.
2) I want more money.
3) I want an uncluttered house.
4) I want a clean and organized garage.

Rather than begin with the dream that has the most negative energy (a perfect body, in this case), I set it aside and work with the one that has the least amount of negative energy (organizing my garage).

I will be more effective if I attempt to clean my garage today than if I try to attain my perfect body. Cleaning the garage carries less negative energy than attaining my perfect body. It will be much easier to achieve and will release whatever negative energy it does contain into a burst of positive energy toward my next dream (uncluttered house). This, in turn will do the same for the next dream (more money), which will do the same for the next (perfect body).

Whatever negative energy is attached to them will dissipate into positive energy upon their achievement. That positive energy will be added to the goals with negative energy, making them easier to achieve.

Remember that I am referring to *today*. The Ultimate Partnership is a one-day-at-a-time operation. Each day our priorities change, often for no apparent reason. In four consecutive days I may end up focusing on all four of my goals. I know the Power guides and adjusts me to achieve all of my goals in the perfect frame of time.

These Priorities Don't Appear To Make Sense

Often, it will happen that your priorities appear illogical considering certain circumstances. You may be in dire need of a refrigerator and yet your gut-level priority at the moment is for a motor boat that you will use only during the summers.

Regardless of the logic (or lack of it), accept your priorities as they are for the day and work with them. They are often mysteriously the means to your other dreams. In looking for the boat, you might happen upon the refrigerator.

Linda U. had her car totaled in an accident. She needed her car for transportation to get to her job. Due to the location of her employment, there was no other means of transportation short of her purchasing another car.

Since she had no other option but to take the next day off, she spent the entire day looking for a car. From 7 a.m. to 10 p.m. she looked everywhere she could, even skipping all of her meals. Finally, that evening she called me. She was frustrated, dejected and full of guilt for having to take another day off work.

After hearing how she handled the first day off, I suggested a different course of action. Instead of searching frantically for a car all day, I suggested she give thanks for a day off and treat it as such; get up leisurely, have a healthy breakfast and ask herself what she feels like doing. Then do it.

She decided to go along with this idea. Her first priority was to sleep later than usual. The next was to eat a good breakfast. After that, she decided to take a nice, long walk.

On her walk she met up with her father. Since the two had not seen each other in a while, they stopped into a restaurant for some coffee and time to talk. The waiter took them to a booth that happened to have a newspaper lying on the table. The paper was opened to (you guessed it) the car ads. One in particular had been circled. An hour later, Linda had a car.

Sometimes the path doesn't look like the path. This is not unusual. It happens to most of us to some degree every single day. What you will find is that all of your visions will eventually manifest with perfect timing. So, don't worry if your priorities don't make sense on a given day. That's the way it works.

Be Specific

Now that you know what you really want and have some priorities set, what do your dreams look like? If you want a new home, where would it be? How many bedrooms? Any particular style? Have you decided to build it yourself or do you want to hire a contractor? Let your mind see the color, the furniture inside, the size of the lot, the feel of the carpet.

As you get more specific about what you want, you will learn more about your own desires. My spouse and I desired to take a cruise. Even though there did not appear to be enough money in our bank account to take the cruise, it still felt like a priority.

The first thing we did was to go to a travel agency that specialized in cruises only. As the travel agent expounded on all of the choices available to us, we realized that we had some very specific preferences.

When did we want to go? Where did we want to go? How long did we want to sail? Did we prefer more sailing time or more port time? Did we want a large ship or a small ship or something in between? Did we want elegance or leisure? Did we want a suite or a regular stateroom? Inside passage or outside passage? We found out that we preferred a quiet, subdued atmosphere to a partying atmosphere. We preferred a trip to the Caribbean rather than one to Alaska (at least this time).

We didn't know what we really wanted until we became specific. The more we concentrated on the particulars, the more excited we became about taking the cruise.

Suddenly, I felt the sensation of the made-up mind. We were going on that cruise. Period. Once I felt this way, I knew beyond a shadow of a doubt that the means to take this cruise would be there one way or another. Our cruise departs in December of 1991 and, as of this writing, we're still in the process of creating this dream. I look forward to meeting some of you on the high seas.

Visualization

The essence of choosing is to envision yourself in the picture of your priority. Daydream! What do you see? How do you feel? What do you hear? Be as detailed as possible.

Surround yourself with mementos of what you want so that you are regularly focusing on your goal. Make it fun. There are some wonderful classes and books available everywhere that can help you with this process. Usually they have the words "Creative Visualization" attached in some way to their titles or subtitles. Check them out. They will be well worth your effort.

They serve to enhance your experience before you have even reached your goal.

Remember, when the mind is made up, there is automatic belief in achievement. When that happens, the Power of the Ultimate Partnership is unleashed, and all things become possible.

Don't Miss The Baritone Hanging On The Wall

Years ago, when I was teaching music in public school, I had a student named Ben who wanted to play the trumpet. My particular program started children in band at the beginning of the sixth grade. Ben was only in the fifth grade and was already setting his Ultimate Partnership in motion. He believed he could be in band, he knew precisely what he wanted to play, and he made his choices clear to me. He even told me he had been envisioning himself playing the trumpet since he was five years old.

Under most circumstances, I would have been tickled to see such enthusiasm in one of my students. But Ben was different. He was confined to a wheelchair, and he was essentially paralyzed from the neck down. He had minimal use of his arms, which were weak, and he had use of his fingers, of which there were only two on his right hand and one on his left hand.

I knew there was no way Ben could manipulate a trumpet. It required too much control from his arms, and his fingers were too far apart to be placed on the valves. Nevertheless, he came to me with a big smile on the first day of sixth grade and said, "I want to play the trumpet." There was a look of absolute joy and certainty on his face.

I suffered intense guilt over this dilemma. I didn't know what to say to him when he came to sign up, so instead, I said, "Come on in and let's see what we can do." As I was walking to the cupboard where the trumpets were kept, I heard him ask, "What's that?"

He was staring up at a shelf on the wall where I had just placed a brand new baritone horn. A baritone horn looks like a concert tuba only much smaller. It sits upright on the player's lap and the mouthpiece naturally meets the player's mouth. I told him what it was and he exclaimed, "I'd rather play that!"

After years of wanting to play the trumpet, he changed his mind in an instant. I realized immediately that he could indeed adapt to the baritone. The horn could be belted to his lap, his arms propped up, and his fingers situated on the valves perfectly. No other control was necessary except learning how to blow into it, and that he could do. He became very proficient on this instrument. The last I'd heard, he had continued on with it through high school.

Ben went after his dream, thinking it was to play the trumpet, and ended up with an even better vision. He never knew that playing the trumpet would have been impossible for him. (Or then again, would it have?)

The message here is this: Go after the dream that you have prioritized without looking for its limitations. If the dream is not the right one for you, a new and better one will come along and replace it automatically. Don't miss the baritone hanging on the wall.

What If My Choices Are Selfish?

Most of us have accepted the false idea that we shouldn't dream for extravagant things because they are selfish. Luxury items such as mansions, expensive sports cars, diamonds, cooks and housekeepers, world travel and even a cool million dollars in cash are dreams that many people think are selfish.

We are so caught up with guilt over wanting abundance in our lives that we have actually convinced ourselves it is wrong to want and have these things. The result of this guilt is that we stifle and hide our desires for the fine life because we have believed we shouldn't want it. Yet, most of us strive for better paying jobs so that we can have it. Do you hear the ridiculousness of this kind of thinking?

One of the arguments against desiring luxury is quoted from the Bible: "If you wish to be complete, go and sell your possessions and give to the poor and you shall have treasure in heaven; and follow me." —Matthew 19:21; "… it is easier for a camel to go through the eye of a needle, than for a rich man to enter the kingdom of God." —Matthew 19:24.

These quotes, read quickly and without real thought, appear to say that if you are wealthy you cannot find God. But let's look at what the words in the first quote are really saying: Jesus is telling us that completeness has nothing to do with money or possessions. That, to discover this fact, we could give everything we own away and we will still experience completeness by following a regimen of love and forgiveness.

In the second quote, Jesus says that it is harder for a rich man to experience this understanding of completeness. The reason for this is that the rich man has more to risk than the poor one, so the poor one will discover the truth of this teaching more easily.

Are you ready to quit your job right now in order to find out if you can still be complete without it? Are you willing to give away even your meager savings account to see if what Jesus said is true? Whatever you are unwilling to give up is what you are rich with. Jesus is really talking about taking risks in order to find happiness. These statements have nothing whatsoever to do with acquiring an abundant life. Indeed, Jesus also said, "I came that they might have life, and might have it abundantly."—John 10:10, and "... everything you ask in prayer, believing, you shall receive."—Matthew 21:22. No qualifiers. Everything.

Direction & Purpose

Here's a new idea to chew on. There is purpose to every one of our desires. Our desires are our instructions. They appear to originate in our own heads, but there is more to it than that. Desire means: de (of) sire (Father)—of the Father, father referring to the creative aspect of God. In other words, the universe exists and functions through order and balance. Each of us has our part to play to keep that order and balance.

Why is it that one of us dreams of being a doctor while the other desires to be an artist? Universal balance. Even Albert Einstein believed in it. He was absolutely convinced that we do not live in a random universe. Our dreams, desires and ideas have been dreamed for us and matched to us. There are reasons, unknown to most of us, for the things we desire, even extravagance.

When any of us purchases something, the money we circulate will eventually be disbursed in some way to everyone. The jewelry shop takes the income from the sale of a diamond ring and pays the jewelry salesperson, who shops for food. The grocery store takes that income and pays the checker, who buys shoes for his daughter. The shoe store chain has decided to donate a generous amount of its profit to fund a crippled childrens' hospital, etc.

Therefore, learn to see your desires as good. Accept that your honest choices, as lofty as they may seem, are for a greater purpose than you or I can see. Your dreams and visions are your directions toward your place in the universal chain. Follow your directions.

RESPONSE #2

Direction

Inspiration, Imagination, Intuition & Incitement

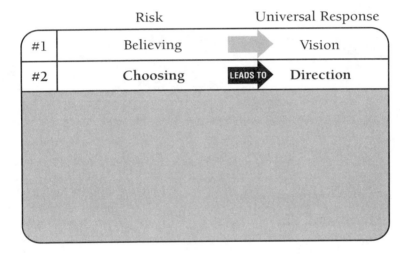

	Risk		Universal Response
#1	Believing	→	Vision
#2	Choosing	LEADS TO	Direction

There was a time in my life when I felt as if I had no direction or purpose. Looking back, I can see that I was stuck within a state of disbelief and impossibility thinking. I had been trying to become what I thought I was supposed to become. I had completely ignored my own dreams, desires and ideas because I did not understand that they were my directions. Once I realized why I was failing at everything, I began to make a few honest choices. I asked myself what I really wanted, even when I was skeptical about my ability to achieve it.

Gradually, I found myself filled with talents and capabilities I had never experienced before. I was creative where I had not been in the past. I came to understand how to achieve my dreams, desires and ideas. As the direct result of making honest choices, I had unveiled the ways and means to achieve them.

I was now presented with clear instructions in the form of the 4 I's: Inspiration, Imagination, Intuition and Incitement. Some of those instructions were contrary to my former perceptions of life. I had been accustomed to feeling doubt, not inspiration; indecision, not imagination; fear, not intuition; and frustration, not incitement. Now I had clear direction.

Once my choices were made, I was given a burst of guidance. So will you. This is how the universe naturally responds to your risk of choosing. It offers you the 4 I's, the ways and means to achieve your goals. You will suddenly find yourself knowing what steps to take, when to take them and how to take them.

This does not mean you will always feel like you are on track. You will simply go about the business of living, and the paths to your dreams will unfold along the way. You will still encounter doubt and indecision, frustration and fear. But the key word to remember is encounter. An encounter is a momentary meeting, not a lifetime venture. You will not *be* doubt and indecision, you will *encounter* doubt and indecision. You will not *be* frustration and fear, you will *encounter* frustration and fear.

As you begin the process of honest choice-making, expect the ways and means to be an abrasive cleansing process. Scraping out your old ideas and ways of life in order to make a place for the new and improved ones may be uncomfortable. This is what makes choosing risky.

Though we will encounter doubt, indecision, frustration and fear along our path, our guidance will not fail us. Inspiration, imagination, intuition and incitement are the ways and means to achieving our goals. They are the fuel that makes the engines of our lives run. Once we have allowed ourselves to believe in possibility, once we have admitted to our real dreams, desires and ideas, we are given the fuel and pointed in the direction of those goals.

Inspiration

Inspiration is the power that shifts our perceptions and emotions to a higher state of awareness. It uplifts the spirit—the consciousness. Have you ever heard anyone say, "All he needs is a little inspiration?" This shift in our perceptions and emotions takes us to a new level of understanding; a more powerful level of understanding.

Inspiration is the booster shot of believing. We need those from time to time as we journey along the path toward our goals. My son has a video game in which the main character periodically collects power pills to keep moving ahead. That's an electronic version of inspiration. We need regular bursts of inspiration to keep us moving forward.

We collect inspiration from every aspect of life. Like the video character, we simply move along the road, solving problems as they arise and relying upon shots of inspiration to be there when we need them. At first the inspiration appears to us in a seemingly arbitrary manner. Then, as we continue along the path, we discover that they are routinely and consistently placed for our greatest good. We came to know where and when to expect them. Soon we seek them out even before embarking upon a new enterprise.

Inspirational people are everywhere. Children, teachers, friends, family members, co-workers, employers, the clergy, movie stars, speakers, fictional characters and total strangers have served as my Power sources. I have been inspired by their words, their actions, their smiles, their excitement and their encouragement.

Inspirational books, periodicals and tapes are plentiful and can be found anywhere from garage sales to department stores. They are often religious or spiritual in nature, but there are many that are completely secular. I keep a variety of them next to my bed so that I can easily reach for one when I encounter doubt, indecision, frustration or fear.

Once, when I was quite upset over my financial situation, I went into the bedroom to meditate and calm down. My books were on a shelf behind me and, without looking at them, I reached back and grabbed one. It was titled *Alter Your Life* by Emmet Fox. I turned to where the bookmark was placed and was startled to find that I was at the beginning of a new chapter: The Magic Of Tithing. Was this just a coincidence? There was a time not too long ago when I would say it was, but not anymore. Tithing was a way to begin solving my financial difficulties. By tithing a regular percentage of my income to my source(s) of spiritual food, I shifted my negative perception about money (not having enough of it) to a positive perception (knowing I would have enough), thereby opening up my possibility thinking.

When I am open to receiving inspiration, I find it in music, art, dance, theater, television, animals, sounds and silence. I could be grocery shopping and overhear a conversation that reminds me of something inspirational. I could be sitting in a park and the sound of a motorcycle will jog the movement of my thoughts and emotions in just the right way to bring up an inspiring idea. I could awaken from a vague dream and be filled with a feeling of encouragement, even though I may not remember anything about the dream. This is the joy of inspiration. It is the gift we receive when we have first risked getting honest about our dreams, desires and ideas.

Imagination

When you have chosen what you want, you will experience a vivid imagination which will help guide you in the pursuit of your dreams. The pictures you see in your head will reflect what you have been choosing. In turn, your imagination will assist you in taking the steps necessary to achieve your dreams.

Imagination automatically follows the experience of inspiration. The more inspired we are, the more vivid our imaginations become. The more we believe in our ability to succeed, the more detail is impressed upon the pictures in our minds.

I once believed that I was not creative. What I did not understand then was that my imagination would flow freely when I became honest about what I really wanted.

For years, I felt mentally and physically paralyzed during special holidays. I would whine and pine that I didn't have enough money to buy my family decent gifts. My friends, on the other hand, all seemed to come up with wonderful ideas for surprising their loved ones with homemade items.

My big excuse was, "I'm just not as creative as all of you are." Poor me. One Valentine's Day I decided (that's another word for "chose") that I was going to make all of my gifts, no matter what. Remember the power of the made-up mind? I came up with incredibly creative ideas that were not only simple but humorous. My family was shocked. So was I.

When I finally became completely honest about what I wanted, my imagination took off. People come up to me today and say things like, "You're so creative. How do you come up with all those ideas?" The truth is they just pop into my head suddenly at the oddest times.

Here's another truth: I have always been imaginative. The reason I didn't feel imaginative was because I didn't take my imagination seriously. I know many people who have wonderful imaginations, but they refuse to believe that there is any reality to them. The result is that they pooh-pooh their own ideas, preferring to trust the ideas of others instead. Of course, another person's idea for your life is just that—another person's idea. This does not mean that others cannot assist us in our revelations. It simply means we should not abandon our own imagination in place of another's.

It's important to look carefully at the images we create. If we keep our dream in mind and soak up inspiration, our images will clearly reflect the steps along the way.

Encountering people with negative attitudes is a signal that, in our minds, we may have been nurturing a negative mental bug. We don't need to purposely hang around its breeding ground. Besides, we're not helping pessimistic individuals by providing them a forum for their negativity.

When the imagination begins to reflect failure, it's time to seek some inspiration to lift us back to a positive level of thought.

That means seeking people who are possibility thinkers. They tend to use terminology that promotes thoughts of success. Listen to the sounds around you. Do you hear "I can'ts" being tossed around? Focus on finding sounds of "I cans" and you will, in no time at all, find yourself past the stage of doubt, indecision, frustration and fear.

By actively seeking inspiration, our imaginations automatically follow suit. Whatever we choose to prioritize and specify, that is what our imaginations will develop. Is your current imagination something you want to see manifested?

Intuition

Have you ever had a feeling about something that you could not validate with concrete evidence? Perhaps you took a longer route to get to the store because it "felt" like the thing to do. Maybe you knew someone was stealing from the till at work but the only proof you had was your gut-level emotion. These are examples of your intuition at work.

Just as inspiration and imagination are natural results of choosing, so is intuition. Inner knowledge is sharpened when we are clear about our dreams, desires and ideas.

Intuition is the inner voice that guides us in the step-by-step direction of our dreams. It is a feeling, a deep understanding of truth that comes from within and is detached from reason, logic and doubt.

Most times, our intuition is perfectly reasonable and logical, but there are times when it doesn't appear that way at all. In these instances, searching for the reason and logic behind intuition creates doubt and distracts us from following it. At these times we are sure there is something wrong with our thinking. All of us have had experiences in which our intuition told us one thing, but we were convinced that it was wrong because it lacked the appearance of reason and logic.

I remember a time when I knew, intuitively, that a co-worker was using drugs at work. There were no obvious outward signs, yet my intuition kept prodding me. This person appeared to be doing very well and I felt silly even thinking such things. Nevertheless, I felt severe apprehension every time I would see him. I believed that if I had mentioned my suspicions to anyone, they would have laughed and said, "That's ridiculous!" Two months later he was caught using marijuana and fired on the spot.

When we feel intuitive about something, but we ignore the intuition, we usually experience a sense of turmoil. This is because intuition is truth. We know some truth, even though there is no way to explain how we know it.

Jack Holland, the director of the Institute for Human Growth and Development in San Jose, California, tells a story about driving a Los Angeles freeway. He was crawling along in his car at a snail's pace as was everyone else. Suddenly he had the thought to get into the right lane. This made no sense whatsoever. It was even more crowded than the lane in which he was already driving. Again the voice commanded, "Get over there!" Again he ignored the voice. Finally, after a third and rather insistent direction, the voice of intuition won its case and Jack moved into the right lane. Immediately, that lane loosened up, but even more astounding was that there was a serious accident in the lane from which he had just moved. Had he not moved, he would have been involved in that accident.

Also, when we ignore intuition and choose to follow a course of action that doesn't feel right, we feel completely misdirected. We are like a ship in the dark, without a lighthouse to guide us. We have no sense of control. We become afraid to make any moves, lest we run aground.

After graduating from high school, I had decided to study music in college. There was one university that stood apart, in my heart, from all the others for no apparent reason. I knew it was where I wanted to go. The doubt, indecision, frustration and fear I encountered was the result of not having the funding to finance my education there. Against my intuition, I decided to enroll in a different, less expensive school.

One month before leaving for college I began to feel terrible. I was overwhelmed with a feeling of impending doom. I could not envision myself at the school I had settled for. I began balking and feeling apathetic toward everything. I had no incentive to pack for school, and I had completely lost interest in studying music.

I talked with my parents about my dilemma. They honored my intuition and made a commitment to do whatever they could to send me to the college of my choice. I felt elated, and I couldn't wait to start school. After notifying the dean of the Conservatory of Music that I intended to enroll, he put me in touch with sources of financing that I had not sought before. I entered the program with scholarships and loans and completed four terrific years there without any financial hardship.

Intuition is the feeling of inner truth. It is the guide. Trusting intuition is trusting ourselves.

Incitement

When your whole body is virtually buzzing with anticipation and you can't wait for the opportunity to move toward your goals, you are experiencing incitement.

Incitement is the steam you receive from the universe when you have combined the spark of inspiration, the substance of imagination and the flow of intuition. You begin to feel a positive forward motion happening in your life, much like the way it feels to ride a locomotive that is just getting started. The track is set and the whistle blows, letting you know there is now enough steam to set your life in motion.

Two years ago, I was introduced to a group of people who were starting a new Toastmasters club. I had never been to a Toastmasters meeting and I had no idea what it was about. Regardless, I enjoyed the company of the other members and saw this as an opportunity for making new friends.

My intuition told me to join the group and I decided to trust my intuition. My alarm clock awakened me at 5 a.m. the following Monday morning in order for me to be at the Toastmasters meeting by 6 a.m. Up until that morning, nothing could convince me of the necessity of arising that early, short of an emergency. Yet, here I was, excited and chipper about my new endeavor and willing to take on a new habit—rising early.

As it turned out, Toastmasters is a terrific organization whose focus is to teach people how to speak in public. At first I followed the format of the meeting just because I wanted to be there. I was enjoying myself immensely. Then I began to appreciate what was happening to me. I learned how to speak without using "uhs" and "you knows" and to stand in front of an audience without quivering and fidgeting. I learned how to put a speech together, how to use gestures and humor, and I became very proficient at timing my speeches.

Five months later, several women asked me if I would teach a class on self-esteem. They were particularly interested in the way I had succeeded at overcoming severe difficulties in my own life. I enthusiastically agreed to teach the class.

Just before the class was to start, the same women asked me if I would use a textbook for the class. I sifted through my huge library of self-improvement books and checked the bookstores and libraries, but I could not find any single book that brought together the same ingredients I used. I had pulled my ideas from all of the helpful books I had read and simplified a process for myself.

Since they wanted me to teach my method, I began writing a 10-week syllabus to use as the text. In the process of putting together the syllabus, I noticed that the format was quite well-organized, and I considered the idea of turning it into a book. That was the birth of my first book, *Pardon My Dust ... I'm Remodeling.*

Here's the significance of my incitement to join Toastmasters: After the book was released, I began to receive invitations to speak everywhere. The more I spoke, the more invitations I received. Today, I do what I've always wanted to do. I write books, give workshops and speak to large audiences everywhere I travel. My incitement to join Toastmasters was the all important ticket toward my life's ambition.

Inspiration, imagination, intuition and incitement—the ways and means to achieving our dreams, desires and ideas; they are given to us full-strength when we risk believing and choosing. Now we come to the third risk, the one that sets the universe in motion around us—action.

The Risk To Take Action

	Risk		Universal Response
#1	Believing	➤	Vision
#2	Choosing	➤	Direction
#3	**Action**		

*C*an you imagine celebrating someone's birthday by merely visualizing the presents being opened or candles being blown out? Of course not. The experience of doing is just as necessary as imaging. Believing in possibility and visualizing a scenario is vitally important to achieving a goal. But it goes nowhere until direct action is taken toward manifesting the scene. Now we move from the realm of idea to the realm of experience—it's party time!

Up to this point, risk-taking has been mental in nature. Believing and choosing are both "inside jobs." If you want to see things change in your life you will have to take action on the 4 I's. All the inspiration, imagination, intuition and incitement is useless unless we act on them.

The universe is responsive to us and cannot move unless there is something to respond to. Remember, this is a Partnership. One part without the other is ineffective. Our part is the action.

Action means making that phone call. It means filling out that application and going to the interview. It means living up to the commitments in your relationships. It means making direct amends for harm done to others. It means giving two weeks' notice at work. It means finding the graphic artist even though you have no money for the printing of your book. It means actively looking for the good in others. It means going on that white water rafting trip. It means doing what your inspiration, imagination, intuition and incitement encourages you to do even though you are afraid to do it. Action means taking risks.

Believing in possibility and choosing what we really want can be uncomfortable. But it is during the risk of action that all of the major terror comes racing to the surface. When we first come to believe in greater possibilities, our intentions are sincere. We honestly want to see these ideas manifest. Everything moves along just fine until we actually have to *do* something to make it happen. Then we suddenly find ourselves stuck. We want to move but our terror disables us. Why? Because of our "what ifs."

"What if" I'm wrong, "what if" this doesn't work, "what if" I lose this or that? We usually don't look beyond these thoughts, even though there is an infinite number of other possibilities. Instead, we stop taking risks. Remember that comfort zone?

We look at the current status of our various situations and guess at their outcomes by virtue of the way they appear to us at that moment. We are so sure we know how everyone is going to react and how everything is going to turn out. We become stubborn in our assessment of reality, falling back into a negative mental picture. When we do this, we immobilize ourselves and nothing in our life changes. We have lots of dreams but we aren't willing to overcome our pessimistic thoughts by taking the action to make those dreams reality. We need some positive perspective.

Perspective

To gain perspective, you must be willing to look at each scenario from an entirely different angle. You must be willing to concede that there are positive avenues and answers, and focus on them instead of the negatives. Getting perspective is like putting on a pair of glasses that allows you to see clearly after you have given up an old pair that has become obsolete. Suddenly you have new vision.

When a mouse is placed in a maze, it starts to run through the maze looking for the cheese. As the mouse runs around one corner it is faced with a wall. It doesn't give up the quest. Nor does it try to beat the wall down. The mouse simply turns about and follows the corridor that's open, even if that corridor seems to take it in the opposite direction of the cheese. The result is that the mouse finds the cheese with little setback. This is the idea behind perspective. Finding the "cheese" means to willingly look for the open corridor and take that route.

It's Your Decision

If you want to move beyond your terror, you must be willing to change your perspective. No one can give you the willingness. You make that decision. Yes, it's hard. It's also hard trudging through life discontented and bored. How long do you want to stay in that condition? What are you willing to do in order to experience a state of contentment and exhilaration now?

These questions will help you get some positive perspective. Using your own risks and your own worst case scenarios (there may be more than one for you), try answering these five questions. See what you come up with:

1) What do you wish you could do that you are afraid to do because you see it as risky?
2) What's the worst that could happen if you took that risk?
3) Do you really believe the worst will happen? (Don't say "I don't know." You do know; in your heart, you do know what you believe.)
4) If the worst happens, will you be destroyed, or will you be able to find an avenue beyond destruction?
5) Describe that avenue.

Here is an example of how I did this concerning my career change:

1) What do you wish you could do that you are afraid to do because you see it as risky?
    Answer: Quit my job today.
2) What's the worst that could happen if you took that risk?
    Answer: I won't find another job that will pay my bills. I'll get

evicted and won't be able to feed my family. We'll be living on the streets.

3) Do you really believe the worst will happen?
   Answer: Probably not.

4) If the worst happens, will you be destroyed or will you be able to find an avenue beyond destruction?
   Answer: I'll find another avenue.

5) Describe that avenue.
   Answer: We will find a place to live, either with friends or family, or a place that is less expensive than what we have now. I will find another job or start my own business. I will build myself back up, this time doing what I enjoy.

I became willing to face the worst possible scenario and gave three weeks' notice to my employer. I went on to start a business in my home that I would never have dreamed possible before quitting my job.

During the transition period, money appeared scarce almost all of the time. It was scary, and I worried and I cried and I whined, and at times, I thought for sure I was crazy to have made the decision to quit. After a while, though, I began to respect myself for my willingness and courage. It ultimately paid off well in many more ways than one.

What I learned from my experience is that there is always some avenue for success, if only I am willing to take the action and stay optimistic. This doesn't mean there won't be fear and anxiety some of the time; it just means that the fear and anxiety is my own invention based on my negative perceptions. The reality is that I will succeed.

From Blaming To Aiming

Another way to overcome our terror is to examine the negative mental statements we make to ourselves that paralyze our ability to act. In other words, how are we blaming? Here is a list of my most common blame statements:

"I can't do that because …
1) my spouse won't let me."
2) first I have to know I have enough money."
3) I'm too fat."
4) it's too hard."
5) you're too busy."
6) he's/she's/they're too intimidating."
7) I'm a woman."
8) I'm not experienced enough."
9) I'm alone."
10) I'm scared to death (frightened into non-existence) over what might happen if I do."

What are your "I can't" excuses? Who or what are you blaming for your refusal to act? Now's the time to get it all out—every excuse, every fear, every lie, every negative idea, every thought of impossibility. They have you paralyzed from taking action. Write them out so you can see your statements face to face:

"I can't do that because …
1) _____ won't let me."
2) first I have to _____ ."
3) I'm too _____ ."

4) it's too _____."

5) you're too _____."

6) he's/she's/they're too _____."

7) I'm a _____."

8) I'm not _____."

9) I'm _____."

10) I'm scared to death (frightened into non-existence) over what might happen if I do."

Don't stop with my examples. Use your own "I can't" statements. List whatever you are blaming for your inability to take prompt action toward your desires.

Now, using your new positive perspective, come up with an "I can" statement to replace each "I can't" statement. This will focus you on the possibilities rather than the impossibilities.

Here are mine:

"I *can* do that because …

1) I believe in the Power of the Ultimate Partnership."

2) I will have everything I need when I need it."

3) I want to."

4) it's my instructions; therefore, it can be done."

5) it's easy."

6) I have the support of my friends and family."

7) I'm a believer, and my mind is made up to succeed."

8) I will learn and grow from the outcome, whatever it is."

9) the outcome will lead me to something better than I had imagined."

10) I choose to do it.

Now it's your turn:

"I *can* do that because ...

1) _____ ."
2) _____ ."
3) _____ ."
4) _____ ."
5) _____ ."
6) _____ ."
7) _____ ."
8) _____ ."
9) _____ ."
10) _____ ."

Doing this will set you on course with your dream, desire or idea. Instead of blaming and remaining stagnant, you will be "aiming" and moving toward your mark.

Be Willing For The Worst To Happen

This next step may bewilder you at first. Try to keep your mind open to it, because it is the key to taking action. Here it is:

Be willing for the worst to happen. Whenever I give this suggestion to people, their first reaction is usually, "No way, José!" and I understand, perfectly, why they feel that way. But let me repeat this suggestion one more time, and this time look carefully at the words:

Be willing for the worst to happen. I didn't say, "Look forward to the worst happening." I said, "Be willing." Any time we get into a car we are willing for the worst to happen. We certainly don't want the worst to happen, but we must be willing or we would never set foot in a car. Christopher Columbus would never have sailed across the Atlantic, Susan B. Anthony would never have marched for women's rights, Neil Armstrong would never have walked on the moon.

This is not to suggest that you have to make headlines; it means that in order to achieve your dreams, you must be willing to experience your fears head on. Otherwise, your fears will hold you hostage to your "what ifs." You will continue along the same path, postponing your happiness indefinitely.

My worst case scenario has happened to me. I risked living in a relationship where I was supporting an active alcoholic/drug addict. I was fired from a public school teaching position as the result of the insanity I was bringing into my work. (Do you have any idea how difficult it is for a public school district to fire a tenured teacher? It's almost unheard of.) This all happened at a time in my life when everything around me was in turmoil.

Losing my job was the most frightening experience I have ever been through, and I will never forget my panic. I had a child to support, a hefty mortgage, car payments, basic home expenses and no income. Neither unemployment compensation nor a $5-per-hour job was going to suffice. I had no skills (I thought) other than teaching music in the public schools.

After three months of waiting, I received a monthly unemployment check that didn't even equal my mortgage. My relationship broke up, and I began managing a popular fast-food restaurant. I despised that job. I am unable to remember a time in my life when I was more miserable. I was lonely, frightened, deeply humiliated and ashamed. Thoughts of suicide were becoming regular visualizations for me. If it wasn't for my son, I might not have chosen to live.

Somehow, all of my expenses managed to get paid. To survive emotionally, I chose to quit the hamburger job and accepted a simple job selling hardware for $5 per hour. It did suffice, though I cannot to this day tell you how.

I began seeking help from recovery groups and therapy. I was sure I would never have the opportunity to teach again due to the reputation I had established. Yet, astonishingly, within one year I was offered (and I accepted) a full-time public school teaching position in another state. I took that as an opportunity to make amends. I did this by practicing positive attitudes and behaviors toward my students and my principals, something I had not done in my past work experience. I had virtually become a new person.

Okay. The worst happened. It was painful. I found help, and my life became better than I ever could have hoped for it to be. The result of "the worst" happening is that I gained experience, knowledge and courage. I learned how to build character in myself, which ultimately became the foundation of my first book. I was able to redefine the meaning of "the worst."

So, in a nutshell, take action on the 4 I's to the best of your understanding of them. You may not always feel like you are on track, but taking action will let you know one way or the other. There is no alternative if you want to experience miracles. The universe awaits your action, and then responds precisely in the way that will bring about your highest good.

RESPONSE #3

The Details

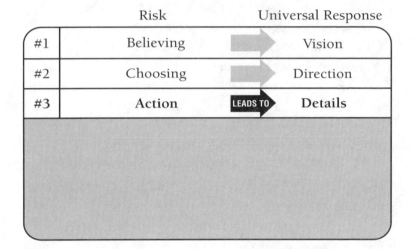

	Risk		Universal Response
#1	Believing		Vision
#2	Choosing		Direction
#3	**Action**	**LEADS TO**	**Details**

Details, details. People, places, timing, money, environment— these are all the details surrounding our dreams, desires and ideas. As we take action on inspiration, imagination, intuition and incitement, all of these details come together harmoniously for our dreams to manifest. This is how the universe responds to the risk of action.

Just for fun, the next time you are introduced to someone, reach out to shake their hand with your left hand instead of your right hand; 99 percent of the time, the other person will respond with his or her left hand. He/she may hesitate for a moment or seem a bit awkward but will still meet you halfway. This is an example of how the universe responds to you when you make a move.

Thoughts also elicit a response from the universe. The thoughts in your head are pure energy. That energy is dispersed as you exercise your thoughts, perhaps even becoming someone else's new thought. Have you ever heard the expression, "You took the words right out of my mouth?" You've probably experienced it many times.

Whether your activity is mental or physical, it is noticed and imprinted upon others who are on the same "wave length." The energy from these thoughts, words and behaviors enters the world around us in a series of vibratory waves, exactly like the waves made by music or by a pebble being dropped in water. There is a ripple effect. It appears as if the waves stop eventually, but what they really do is continue on, acting and reacting upon other waves. A form of communication takes place.

The energy that we disperse unifies harmonically with the energy from the universe, which begins to conform to our needs. This is how the details begin working together to manifest our visions.

When Marconi invented the wireless telegraph (otherwise known as the radio), his success came one day before another inventor in England succeeded, using the exact same principles. Neither of them knew the other was working on this project. It is believed that, since both were focused on finding the same answer, when one discovered something, his thoughts grasped onto the thoughts of the other. They were actually substantiating each other's theories along the way without even knowing it.

Objects also have a vibratory rate. Rocks and steel, which appear to be solid, are not solid at all. They consist of molecules that are continuously moving. The rate at which they move determines the nature of the object. All things are subject to reacting to all other things, though we haven't yet learned precisely how this works.

When my spouse and I decided to move to Oregon in 1984, there was a recession going on in the state. Our friends all warned us that we would "be back within three months." We had learned to follow our intuition, and it was telling us to make the move anyway. We made the decision and gave notice to our employers. We sold our furniture and packed up the cars in preparation for the move.

Neither of us had applied for jobs in Oregon, and I figured I would pick up temporary work while seeking another teaching position. Two days before we were to leave, I received a phone call from a school district in the Portland area. (I had submitted my resumé to that district three years earlier but had not maintained contact with them.) The woman on the phone informed me that there was an opening for a Jr. high/Sr. high orchestra teacher and "would it be possible for you to interview for this position Wednesday morning at eleven?" We had planned to arrive in Portland on Tuesday evening.

The story, up to this point, is an excellent example of how the universe responds to us automatically when we make a decision and take direct action toward our goals. But the rest of the story is so incredible I just don't want to leave it out.

As I mentioned before, they were seeking an orchestra director. My specialty was choral music and band. I was not trained to teach an orchestra. When I arrived for the interview, I was informed that I was the 25th person in two months interviewed for this job. I thought to myself, "That's very strange. Surely there were a few qualified orchestral teachers out of 24 applicants. Why would they even consider a band director?"

Nevertheless, the interview continued, and I was told to call them the next morning for their decision. I really wanted that job, and I believed I was going to get it. I knew I could teach an orchestra quite well, even though my paper qualifications didn't indicate that fact. When I called them the next morning, they said, "We would be honored if you would accept this orchestral position."

So far, the universe was responding right on time—and it was not finished just yet. In Oregon, it is complicated to obtain a teaching credential. Certification requirements are quite substantial. The forms must be filled in and submitted, my educational transcripts from college had to be ordered, and, in the event that I did not have the necessary course work for certification, I would have to complete whatever was missing before my certificate could be issued. In other words, if I didn't qualify, I couldn't teach. The process usually takes from three to six months. Our decision to move to Oregon had been a spur-of-the-moment decision. I had not prepared for my teaching certificate.

Instead of three months, it took less than two weeks to get all of the paperwork completed and evaluated. I was missing two major courses that I would need to become certified. I had already been offered a job and would not be able to accept it—I thought. After informing my supervisor of this dilemma, she told me to wait by the phone for one hour. Within the hour I received a call from the certification department informing me that they were sending me my certificate. The courses I needed had been waived. Apparently, the superintendent of this school district called the state department of education and pulled some strings.

All this for a band director who appeared not even to have the qualifications to teach orchestra.

I doubt that I am the only one who has experienced these kinds of incredible coincidences. Haven't you experienced people, places, timing, money, environment and other details coming together even when it seemed incomprehensible for them to do so?

Just as our belief in a successful move to Oregon culminated in the choices we made surrounding that move, our decision to act on our choices culminated in the responses we received from people, places, timing, money and environment. The better we get at listening and following our 4 I's, the easier life seems to be.

Now—there is a gray area that can be confusing if you do not understand the concept of people and things responding to one another's vibrations. This gray area concerns the appearance of the details. They don't always appear to be leading us to our goals along the way. Remember the story of Linda U., who found the car she needed by taking a leisurely walk; and I found the graphic artist for this book when I was in the process of renting cross-country skis. Believe it or not, this is really the norm instead of the exception.

Examine your own life, and you will probably find many more occasions when you found what you were looking for when and where you least expected. However, we don't realize this happens because it is so common. And, when we really want something desperately, we tend to obsess about finding it.

At these times, we are acutely aware of the details looking chaotic. Money and timing are the details that disturb us the most, especially when they don't conform to our expectations. Regardless of our perception, the fact remains that the details are working just fine. The best thing we can do is to concentrate on working with them rather than working to change them. The next risk shows us how to do this.

RISK #4

The Risk To Practice Integrity

	Risk		Universal Response
#1	Believing	➡	Vision
#2	Choosing	➡	Direction
#3	Action	➡	Details
#4	**Integrity**		

*I*ntegrity is one of the most important, yet misunderstood words in the English language. It is most often used interchangeably with honesty, though there is much more to it than that. From Webster's New World Dictionary: *Integrity*: "the quality or state of being complete, whole, unimpaired, sound." *Integrate*: "to make whole or complete by adding or bringing together parts." You've heard people claim they were "falling apart" over something or other. They are lacking integrity because they are missing one or more of the pieces that integrates them into wholeness.

We gain integrity by bringing together three elements that make us whole—honesty, generosity and goodwill. All three elements of integrity must be practiced collectively and unconditionally. Honesty without generosity and goodwill is nothing more than blame and judgment. Generosity without honesty and goodwill is little more than people-pleasing and co-dependency. And goodwill without honesty and generosity is usually selfish will ("I wish for you what I think you ought to have, even if you don't want it.").

Integrity is a risk because it means putting our best attitudes and behaviors forward at the very moments we want to do the opposite. These elements are described and defined in depth in *Pardon My Dust ... I'm Remodeling*, however, a brief description of each will suffice for the purpose of this book.

First Element: Honesty

Whatever is the truth in any way, to the best of your understanding, is honesty. Whatever is not stealing, cheating or deception in any way, to the best of your knowledge, is honesty. I am talking about unconditional honesty—gracious honesty, no matter what.

Whatever thoughts leave you feeling compassionate, kind, loving and understanding are honest thoughts. The truth sets us free from worry, anger, resentment, fear and depression. So, if what you are thinking about people, places, timing, money and environment (the details) is causing you to experience worry, anger, resentment, fear and depression, you have not found the truth. Re-think. Create new thoughts that feel compassionate, kind, loving and understanding. Then you will have found truth. You will be building integrity through self-honesty.

It's all very simple. And it may appear very risky. Getting this honest seemed impossible to me until I found out that there are many people who actually practice it meticulously. When I finally made the decision to apply this kind of honesty to my life (to the best of my understanding), I learned what integrity really felt like. Are you ready, willing and able to experience unconditional honesty?

Second Element: Generosity

Generosity means showing up to that meeting. It means saying yes to a call for assistance. It means letting go of money even when you are afraid you won't have enough for yourself. The root meaning of generosity is to produce, bring into being, cause to be. What do you generate in the world? What do you produce? What do you create life within? Generosity is characterized by circulation. Blood circulates, and there is life. People circulate by attending classes, parties, special interest groups and organizations. In the process they are giving of themselves so that all may have a good time.

If you want to practice the integrity principle of generosity, ask yourself a simple question: Am I more concerned with what I am going to get from others, or am I more concerned with my capacity to be of service to others?

When I am giving time, money, service and love to others with honesty and goodwill as my motivators, I am practicing generosity. But when I am doing things for others because I want them to treat me better, or when I am doing things for others because I'm afraid not to do them, I am not truly generous. I am people-pleasing and manipulative. If there is any expectation after the giving, there is no integrity. Real generosity is giving without strings—any strings.

Again, it's all very simple. And it's all very risky. It means examining my attitudes and behaviors around money issues, time and service to others. Are you ready, willing and able to experience this kind of generosity?

Third Element: Goodwill

Goodwill means wishing the best for others and seeing the best in others, no matter who they are or what they may have done. It means finding the seed of good in every circumstance, no matter how negative it may appear at the moment.

This is the essence of what is commonly called forgiveness and love. Forgiveness and love are manifested automatically by the practice of goodwill. Practice goodwill unconditionally, and you'll experience a sense of power unlike anything you have ever felt. Are you ready, willing and able to replace negative attitudes with goodwill?

Integrity And The Details

We are most likely to abandon integrity principles when the details (people, timing, money, etc.) don't appear to be leading us toward our vision. We "fall apart" (lose integrity) by becoming dishonest, greedy and ill-willed in order to manipulate situations to "go our way." Not only do we practice these deceptions with others, but with ourselves as well (surely, we are fooling ourselves to think that anything comfortable could come through dishonesty, greed and ill will).

My mom (who is very proud of her daughter—the *author*) called a local bookstore to see if *Pardon My Dust …* was in stock. Instead of simply asking if the store carried that title, she pretended to be interested in buying it. She was afraid they would think she was being pushy about her daughter if she told them the real reason she called. They immediately asked her if she wanted them to hold the book for her. She stammered that she already had the book but was calling for "a friend." They then asked for her "friend's" name so they could hold it for her "friend." Again, she stammered that she had to check with her "friend" first. She called me to tell me about this humorous situation and we both laughed. One of the main emphases of *Pardon My Dust …* is unconditional honesty.

There was a time when I told many white lies. I believed I was justified in doing this because I thought I was sparing someone's feelings, and/or I thought I was protecting myself. I was mistaken on both counts. Whoever I was "sparing" could feel my deception, which probably felt even worse than the truth itself. Also, telling white lies invited interrogation from people who had good enough instincts to question my sincerity. That interrogation was definitely not protection.

We get scared when we can't see how something is going to work. All of our lives we've heard the expression, "Seeing is believing." Now we are asked to "Believe, and then we'll see." Part of believing is letting the Power of the Ultimate Partnership take care of the details. We do this by acting on inspiration, imagination, intuition and incitement, and then we step back and allow the details to piece together.

What If My 4 I's Are Telling Me To Be Dishonest, Greedy or Ill-willed?

Occasionally during my workshops, someone will say, "My inner voice (intuition) told me to lie." This is not intuition at all. This is merely the ego responding to fear. Lying is the way we attempt to protect ourselves.

The way to know the difference between your voice of fear (ego) and your 4 I's is simple: your 4 I's always reflect integrity (honesty, generosity and goodwill). The frightened ego always reflects dishonesty, greed and ill will. When this is understood, you will be able to distinguish between the two; then you can risk practicing integrity when your ego is nudging you to do otherwise. That's when you will experience the miracles of the Ultimate Partnership.

It is no miracle to win through cheating; nor does it feel fulfilling. There is no awe in watching the bills get paid as the result of greediness; only a false sense of security, nothing else. There is no realization of happiness through hatred, fear or resentment; just the dubious sweetness of revenge.

Any real inspiration, imagination, intuition or incitement that we receive will guide us with honesty, generosity and goodwill. This is how we can be sure of our decisions. If they lead us to integrity, they are a good bet to act upon. Otherwise we are better off waiting for clearer insight.

What Does Integrity Do To Help The Partnership Work?

Practicing integrity assures that the details progress without interruption. This is ultimately the fastest pace, even though it may not appear to be. We often think that, if we manipulate the details, they will work better; that the outcome will be better for us. Not so. When we practice dishonesty, greed or ill will, we slow down the natural process even though we think we are actually speeding things up. We may succeed in attaining a goal or two along the way through a breech of integrity, only to find we have detoured from the more significant goal.

Probably the most important reason to practice integrity is to experience the reality of the Ultimate Partnership. It works. It really works. If you are spending your time trying to push and cajole the details to fit your own idea of what they should look like, you will never experience this incredible process.

Chris A. worked at a very well-known athletic clothing corporation. As an employee, she was allowed to shop at the employee store, which sold the athletic clothing at a substantial discount. While family members of the employees were eligible to purchase from this store, friends were not. Chris was single and believed this rule to be unfair to single employees.

For ten years, Chris brought her friends into the store, claiming that they were family members. In 1990, Chris was introduced to the integrity principles. She was trying to make some positive changes in her life at the time, and this looked like the place to start. After reading *Pardon My Dust* ..., Chris made a list of those areas in her life that were missing integrity. The employee store was at the top.

She made an appointment with the manager of the employee store and made herself ready to make amends. As she straightforwardly gave him an account of the past ten years, she worried about being fired. When she was finished, the manager sat back incredulously. He told her he had never met such an honest person and that he admired her courage. He also thanked her for her input about single employees. Then he promptly told her that she was welcome to bring any of her friends to the employee store from that time on.

With integrity, even the smallest accomplishments are major victories. A small accomplishment, achieved while taking the risk of practicing unconditional integrity, feels as miraculous as a larger accomplishment. Honesty, generosity and goodwill add up to a life of health, prosperity and happiness—miracles.

RESPONSE #4

Miracles

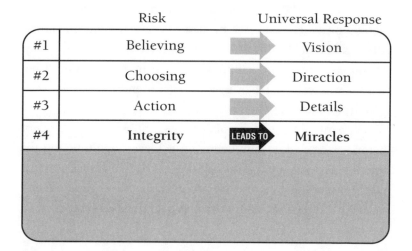

	Risk		Universal Response
#1	Believing		Vision
#2	Choosing		Direction
#3	Action		Details
#4	**Integrity**	**LEADS TO**	**Miracles**

We have believed and experienced vision. We have chosen and experienced direction. We have acted and experienced the details responding to us. We have kept our integrity and now we are about to experience miracles.

When we are astounded over the unexpected, even to a slight degree, we experience the feeling of the miracle. Integrity creates the experience of the unexpected because it requires us to walk a straight line even though the ground around us appears to be shaking.

At first we are sure we are going to fall or be swallowed up by a crack in the earth. Eventually, the shaking stops. Looking around we find ourselves in new and improved territory. "Wow!" we think. That's the experience of a miracle.

At this writing, my son Corey is 11 years old. Up until this year, he had exhibited no interest in playing team sports. He enjoyed karate, roller-skating, swimming and other sports that didn't require team participation. Recently, he decided to join his school's basketball team. After the first two practices he was questioning his decision. He felt like a fish out of water, and the other players were often impatient with him. After contemplating the situation, he decided to stick it out for at least six practices and one game.

By the time those practices were over and one game had been played, Corey had decided to keep playing. He spent three-quarters of the season just learning how to play the different positions. One of his dilemmas was that no one would throw the ball to him. Soon, he realized that in order to get the ball, one must be in a good position to receive it. He became more and more aggressive each time a game was played. By the end of the season, Corey was getting the ball.

His fears of being "swallowed up" by the team were only subject to his attitude. Once he took some risks, the team responded positively. The season ended with a pizza party, and Corey came home with the first trophy he had ever received.

For Corey, this was a miracle. Without his willingness to take a risk (action) and stick with the team (integrity), subjecting himself to his worst fears (the judgments of his peers), he would have missed out on the miracle.

The Vision Begins To Manifest

After you practice integrity, you will begin to see your vision come to fruition, either in whole or in part. This is the miracle. In other words, you will begin to receive or experience what you have been desiring.

The dream of a college education begins with the belief in possibility (Risk #1). We discover multitudes of educational programs to choose from (Response #1). From them, a specific program of study is chosen (Risk #2). We are directed by the 4 I's, inspiration, imagination, intuition and incitement (Response #2). We apply to the colleges we would like to attend (Risk #3). The details of people, places, timing, money and environment begin to support the vision (Response #3). We do our own work and make our own grades (Risk #4). We receive our college diploma (Response #4).

When the miracle appears, we realize that all of the difficult risk-taking is behind us. Miracles build character because they awaken us to the fact that there are possibilities beyond our present comprehension. They stretch our imagination, strengthen our faith in our abilities, and they lead us to greater good.

RISK #5

The Risk To Acknowledge

	Risk		Universal Response
#1	Believing	➤	Vision
#2	Choosing	➤	Direction
#3	Action	➤	Details
#4	Integrity	➤	Miracles
#5	**Acknowledgment**		

The next risk in the process of manifesting our dreams, desires and ideas is the risk of acknowledgment. Acknowledgment is the mastery of staying awake while we live. That may sound funny to you, but the fact of the matter is that most of us are asleep while the miracles of our lives are happening.

I'm not talking about physical sleep. I'm referring to mental sleep; the kind that is best described by the word *oblivious*. We are lacking active conscious knowledge of what is taking place in our lives.

The result of this cognitive slumber is that we miss the

enjoyment of watching our dreams under construction. We lose track of all of the miracles that happen because most of them seem insignificant. We forget to notice the car working properly, the little bills getting paid, the food in the cupboards or the kids getting home safely each day from school.

In essence, we have been oblivious to the moment-by-moment process of living. We have been so focused on the outcome that we have missed the miracle in the making. Each achievement along the way is the vision manifesting itself. By acknowledging the pieces of our visions as they manifest, we keep awake to the fact that the dream is now the reality.

There are several reasons why people find it difficult to acknowledge the the pieces of their miracles. Here are some of the most common ones:

It's "Bad Luck"

Acknowledging one's blessings is risky business for some people. They are superstitious. They have a difficult time acknowledging when something wonderful has happened to them because they think, if they say how good it all is, they will lose it. They have no problem pointing out how well others have done, but when it comes to their own blessings, they minimize their value.

My grandmother and her sisters were quite superstitious about admitting that they felt well. They had a regular weekly contest to see which of them was the sickest. Whoever had to take the most pills seemed to be the "winner." Though it went unsaid, the idea behind it all was that it was good luck to say you were sick—especially when you weren't.

One day, while engaged in one of their matches, my grandmother suddenly recognized the insanity of their conversation. After one of my great aunts had proven herself to be the sickest, my grandmother looked at me and quipped, "Boy, am I jealous!"

Too Ordinary

Another reason people refuse to acknowledge the miracles is because they don't recognize a miracle when they see one. They are not impressed with the nature of the manifestation, so they don't see it as anything miraculous.

For example, I get up in the morning with my son, see him off to school, and rarely acknowledge the fact that he knows how to coordinate colors when he dresses. This everyday occurrence did not seem miraculous until the day he came out of his bedroom wearing red pants and an orange shirt. Suddenly I found myself acknowledging his coordinated choices more often.

Another time I almost missed a miracle was when I was running late for a speaking engagement. I was due at a luncheon at noon, but I was still downtown at a shopping mall. I needed to use the rest room before leaving for the luncheon, and I chose one that I thought would be somewhat empty. Instead, there was a long line. I began to get huffy about having to wait. Though I looked perfectly calm on the outside, in my head I was tapping my foot impatiently and had my arms crossed angrily.

As I glanced behind me to see how much longer the line was becoming, a woman recognized me and shouted, "I know you!

You're that author." She then went on and on telling everyone how she had seen me on television and in the newspaper, and how much my book had helped her. What publicity! If the line hadn't been long, I would have missed this opportunity to be noticed. I promptly acknowledged the miracle and vowed to be more awake in the future.

Not Seeing The Parts As Equaling The Whole

As I pointed out earlier, all of the joys of risk-taking are, in themselves, small manifestations of our dreams. Until we understand this, we tend to be oblivious of the stepping stones that lead us across the river.

The experience of a vacation begins with the belief that a vacation is possible. With that belief comes the joy of vision. Having a focused vision for one's vacation is a great accomplishment. Without the vision, there would be no vacation. Along with a specific vision comes the ways and means—the inspiration, imagination, intuition and incitement—the direction for accomplishing the vacation. Receiving the 4 I's is a great achievement. They promote the right action to take. The action we take leads to the details coming together. They are the miracles surrounding the ways and means. Our persistence and integrity leads to a satisfying outcome.

Some of the miracles we might take for granted and never notice are: the whole family agreeing on vacation plans; everyone getting the same time away from their jobs; the cabin reserved; the fishing equipment fitting in the car; enjoying the scenery along the way. These are all vital parts of the experience of a vacation.

Other miracles are disguised as impossible situations: nobody is able to agree on vacation plans; no one can coordinate vacation dates; all of the cabins are rented; the fishing equipment was washed away when the river flooded last summer; there was so much rain, the scenery was not visible. How are these misfortunes equivalent to miracles? They are like the grooves that keep the needle on a record. There is guidance. Maybe, just maybe, the alternatives to the originally desired plans are better; but until we are forced to find alternatives, we don't realize it.

If each miracle is acknowledged as a necessary part of the larger vision (the experience of a successful vacation), then the momentum and Power of the Ultimate Partnership is enhanced. Our choices are more easily visualized, direction is clearer, action is easier, the details are smoother, integrity comes naturally, and the whole process feels more miraculous. We then have a great vacation instead of just a good vacation.

I went to a weekend retreat at the coast a few years ago, and I had a fabulous time. I made new friendships, rested, contemplated, experienced new sensations and grew in understanding of myself and others. I had so much fun that I did not want the weekend to be over. In the past, I would have spent the last day pining over what I was losing now that the fun was ending. My joy would have ended before the finale of the retreat.

This time, instead of focusing on the fact that I was leaving the fun behind, I spent the last day acknowledging all of the fun moments and creating more of them. Now I could relive the joyful feelings over and over and bring that joy into all of my new experiences.

Ways To Acknowledge

There are innumerable ways to acknowledge our miracles as they occur. First, we must get used to looking for them when they are not obvious. It's easy to pinpoint the miracles that feel good; we usually acknowledge them as they are happening. The goal is to root out those miracles that are camouflaged and/or disguised in such a way that we don't recognize them as miracles.

One of my favorite ways to do this (and also a very effective way at that) is to examine some area in my life where there is conflict. I ask myself, "Where am I angry? Where am I disappointed? Where am I hurt? Where am I sad? Where am I frustrated? Where am I fearful? Where am I pessimistic? Where am I judgmental? Where am I embarrassed? Where am I ashamed? Where am I skeptical? Where am I sarcastic? Where am I depressed? Where am I apathetic? Where am I anxious?"

Wherever there is conflict in my life, there is a miracle waiting to be discovered; and this is the way I discover it:

I Become Willing To See The Miracle
and
I Look For It

Here is an example of this technique from my own experience:

I was flying down to Fresno, California, to do a couple of workshops. My travel agent assured me that he would book my flights on regular-sized commercial jets and find me the quickest route to my destination.

When I received the non-refundable tickets in the mail, I found two disturbing conditions. One was that I would be flying on a small commuter airplane for half of the trip. Having just overcome a paralyzing fear of flying on regular-sized jets, I was not quite ready to tackle the small commuter planes. The other disturbing condition was that there was a three hour stopover in Salt Lake City, Utah. I am not fond of sitting in airports for hours with little to do.

When I found out that my travel agent could have placed me on a flight that met my original expectations, I was angry, fearful and disgusted. This kind of predicament does not fare well for me when I'm on my way to do workshops on positive attitudes. Nevertheless, I was determined to admit these circumstances were miracles just bursting to show themselves, and I was willing to look for them.

My spouse and I boarded the regular-sized jet and flew to Salt Lake City. Once there, we searched for something to keep us occupied. We decided to take a walk outside the terminal building. There we found a hotel limousine waiting to take patrons from the airport to a downtown hotel. The driver told us that he could give us a ride downtown if we promised to eat lunch at the restaurant within that establishment. We agreed. Within the next three hours we had a terrific lunch, took a tour of the Mormon Temple, heard the Mormon Tabernacle Choir as they sang in the Tabernacle, visited the central office of a major bookstore, enjoyed a leisurely stroll on a beautiful day in a lovely town and got back to the airport just in time to board our flight into Fresno. I felt great, and the week in Fresno was highly successful.

The ride home was on an airplane that sat 19 people and looked more like a mosquito than an airplane. Our seats were located in the very back of the plane, and I was absolutely terrified. I came to find out that the seats we had were, for that kind of plane, the very best ones. They were roomy (as much as could be expected, considering the size of the mosquito ... er ... plane), and they were situated behind the roar of the engines so our eardrums were not numbed during the flight. As it turned out, that flight was smoother and more enjoyable to me than the flight on the regular-sized jet.

So, I had a wonderful opportunity to visit a town where I had never been, and I overcame another fear. I had discovered the miracles hidden in the crises.

What are your crises? The Chinese view the term *crisis* as a problem and an opportunity all rolled into one. Can you find the opportunities within tragedies as well as the little disturbances? Are you ready and willing? Once you can find miracles in the pain, you'll begin to see them everywhere. When this happens for you, a whole new world will open itself up for your personal enjoyment. The next step is to actively practice acknowledgement of those miracles. Gratitude is one good way to start.

Gratitude

Expressing gratitude is one process of acknowledgment. As we begin to see everything as a blessing, we view the world from the angle of opportunity. Every challenge can be considered another avenue for personal growth. Instead of complaining when our comfortable little world shakes underfoot, we give a thought or word of thanks for the opportunity to grow.

Recently, my car broke down in the middle of a busy intersection. Previously, I would have become angry, frustrated and somewhat fearful. This time I was ready to practice gratitude. I began by thanking the universe for an opportunity. Just what that opportunity was, I could not comprehend; nevertheless, I watched for the opportunity.

Soon, I realized that my son was watching me as I worked

through the dilemma. Here was one opportunity; it was a chance for him to observe a healthy role model. He watched me as I gave gratitude, smiled and said, "I wonder what miracle we're going to be introduced to." He responded in like manner.

We took a walk to the nearest phone. I called my insurance carrier and was told the tow truck would be about an hour. The tow truck was there in less than 15 minutes: miracle #1. The problem was a loose battery connection that was fixed in less than five minutes: miracle #2. Thank you, universe.

Expressing gratitude as a form of acknowledgment also creates open and appreciative relationships with others. I have heard many complaints from people who feel unappreciated at their jobs because the boss never says thanks, and vice versa. The same applies to our families and friends. A simple note or card of acknowledgment can do wonders for everyone involved. It clears the air for greater intimacy and trust; and it doesn't have to be from the head honcho—it can be to the head honcho.

Say It Loud: I'm Blessed And I'm Proud!

Sharing an accomplishment with a friend or a stranger is another effective means of acknowledging. For one thing, before you verbalize, you visualize. You get to reinforce your own memory of the accomplishment, which serves to stimulate greater amazement and belief in the Power of the Ultimate Partnership. That in turn stimulates greater visions.

Also, when the verbalizing of the miracle is coming from a heart filled with gratitude, it serves as testimony for unlimited possibility thinking. The person who hears this testimony becomes inspired.

Acknowledgment of any kind serves as testimony that the achievement of dreams, desires and ideas is infinitely possible.

For this reason, acknowledgment is an indispensable commodity. As we openly acknowledge our miracles, we become a vital force for others' achievements. We begin to understand that our lives have purpose. *We suddenly realize that, as we dream and respond to others' dreams—together—we are the Power of the Ultimate Partnership.*

RESPONSE #5

The Student Appears

	Risk		Universal Response
#1	Believing	➤	Vision
#2	Choosing	➤	Direction
#3	Action	➤	Details
#4	Integrity	➤	Miracles
#5	**Acknowledgment**	**LEADS TO** ➤	**Students**

As each of us acknowledges our achievements and miracles, the universe acknowledges us right back. Comments are made to us from various individuals, and suddenly we find ourselves surrounded by people who want to achieve as we have. They are essentially our students.

What is a student? Well, all of us are perpetual students of life. Any time we have curiosity or interest about anything, we take on the role of student.

Obtaining students is not a choice—it is a result. When we voice our accomplishments, we are automatically presented with students. These students are the people who listen to us as we are engaged with them in a friendly chat; they are the individuals who overhear our conversation from another table in a restaurant. They could be next-door neighbors, family members, friends, co-workers, employers, employees or complete strangers.

Their interest is not nosiness, though it may appear to be that way. Rather, they are attracted to whatever they are hearing because they are on a specific path that includes something we are sharing. Have you ever had someone say, "Excuse me, I wasn't meaning to listen in on your conversation but you said something that caught my ear ..."? Have you ever been the one listening in?

What people are actually receiving from us is the ways and means; the inspiration, imagination, intuition and incitement to go on believing and achieving. In this case, we play the part of direction. Together, we are the Power of the Ultimate Partnership, working with and for one another.

Our initial acknowledgment or testimony is usually natural. It happens as the result of our own amazement and astonishment at having manifested a miracle. We don't say to ourselves, "Okay, now I'm going to find a student with whom I will share my miracle." What really happens is that a "student" will come up to us at some point and tell us how much we helped them when we shared some aspect of our achievements.

We experience incredible joy when that happens. This is when we begin to see the purpose to our lives. We suddenly realize that there is a web connecting us to everyone in the world. An inspiring account from me to one other person will be told and retold, each time helping to guide another student.

Most of the time, we have no idea who these students are going to be; and when we do learn who they are, it is very often surprising. Recently, I was invited to be the keynote speaker at a meeting where there were about 50 people in attendance. I was to speak for 45 minutes concerning the concepts in *Pardon My Dust ... I'm Remodeling*.

I noticed a gentleman in the front row who was slumped in his chair. His arms were crossed tightly, his legs were stretched out rigidly and also tightly crossed, he had a frown on his face, and he looked wholeheartedly disgusted. I was talking about generosity of spirit and unconditional goodwill. I've learned to ignore appearances in order to keep up the momentum of my talks; but I couldn't help thinking that this guy would rather be stuck in a hornets' nest than be listening to me.

After my talk was over and the meeting was adjourned, this man hurried up to me and hugged me. I had almost expected that he was going to punch me in the nose. Instead, he thanked me for the most inspiring talk he had ever heard. He then went on to tell me that he had been a real grouch at home and at work. He was now on his way to the florist to present his office staff with flowers and an invitation to take them all out for lunch that day. Then he was going to the travel agent to make vacation plans in Hawaii for himself and his wife. He said my talk had convinced him that he had misplaced his priorities.

Can you imagine how I felt after hearing all of that? There is a pleasant kind of shock value when I realize that my testimony is useful to others, even when it isn't obvious. It's what keeps me moving forward during times of stress and uncertainty. It reminds me that I do make a difference.

My books are my acknowledgments of my miracles. They attract students who are seeking similar answers. Receiving letters from readers who live in places I've never heard of is downright invigorating. Just one letter from someone sharing with me what he or she is striving toward is enough to put me on Cloud Nine for a week. This joyful experience happens to everyone who believes, chooses, acts, exercises integrity and practices acknowledgment.

The natural result of sharing our miracles and acknowledging our accomplishments is realizing we have students. When we were just beginning to acknowledge our miracles, we were somewhat unconscious of that fact. Now we are aware that what we experience and share with others makes a difference. The next step is to openly teach what we know about achieving our visions.

R I S K #6

The Risk To Teach

	Risk		Universal Response
#1	Believing	➤	Vision
#2	Choosing	➤	Direction
#3	Action	➤	Details
#4	Integrity	➤	Miracles
#5	Acknowledgment	➤	Students
#6	**Teaching**		

A rose bush begins with a seed that is filled with incredible possibilities. From looking at that seed, one would never know the capacity of knowledge amassed within. It has a vision of itself imprinted in its memory, and, as it burrows itself in the soil, its roots are directed toward food and water. Once it has a strong foothold in the earth, it begins to branch toward the sunlight. It cooperates with the details of weather, soil conditions and temperature. Finally, it breaks through the soil and into the air. The entrance of the seedling into the light is its acknowledgment of itself to the world. And in return, the world acknowledges and learns from it.

We are the same as the rose. We come into this life filled with unlimited possibilities. Those of us who fully realize this fact are filled with vision. We see ourselves as we want to be, and we begin to choose. When those choices are made, we become directed. As we follow our directions, working with the details and keeping integrity, our visions are manifested in miraculous ways. We acknowledge our miracles because most of the time we cannot contain our excitement. The students begin to appear, and we realize we are teachers.

It was never a choice to accumulate students; this happens naturally as we achieve and acknowledge our achievements. It is a choice to teach. At first our students learned from us by observation. We had no idea we were teaching and inspiring others. Now we have come to realize that our successes have benefits for others. We are at a conscious awareness of people listening and learning from us. Now the real risk of teaching is at hand.

Stolen Ideas

There are many potential teachers who do not want to share the secrets of their success. They are afraid others will "steal" their ideas. They fear that others will capitalize on their vision and do better or look better than they do. This presents a risk because their egos want them to be better than anyone else.

What they may not realize is that letting go of an idea so that others may benefit from it releases an incredible amount of energy for the creation of newer ideas. It is well-understood in recovery circles that sharing our successes with others helps us to make our own successes more stable.

IBM designed and developed a new computer that was easier for lay people to use. The patent on the invention lasted for years, holding back progress and increased creativity. Once the patent ran out and other companies could clone the original, IBM suddenly became more creative and developed the PS/2, an even better idea. This has happened many times in the business world. Once everyone has access to an idea, it seems that bigger and better ideas pour forth.

Jealousy

Part of teaching is openly acknowledging our students' achievements. This is a risk because it threatens the ego. When we realize our students are becoming respected as teachers also, there is a temptation to become manipulative. We will withhold information about them or minimize their success. We may take advantage of our positions of authority to keep another person from moving ahead or gaining popularity. We may fear losing the status of guru if our students achieve more than we do.

Also, when we suspect that our students are learning quickly, we may attempt to lead them off course. An acquaintance of mine was having wonderful success at staying on a food plan and releasing her excess weight. I overheard her as she was sharing her exultation with her "teacher," who was not doing as well. Her teacher said to her, "Don't get too excited, you're bound to fail shortly, everybody does."

Integrity plays an important part of continued success at this point in the cycle of achievement. As teachers, we must—with goodwill—wholeheartedly and openly support our students, and other teachers as well.

An author friend (who writes and teaches similar concepts to mine) recently came into an inheritance that is allowing her to publicize her book very effectively. She purchased a rather expensive booth at a major booksellers convention and is sharing it freely with at least three other authors who have not manifested enough funds to do the same. I am one of them. She is well aware that the support and encouragement she lovingly and willingly gives others can only strengthen her own success.[1] This is how the Power of the Ultimate Partnership becomes magnified.

Teaching Our Own Truths

Truth is indeed stranger than fiction. When we are seeking a particular goal, we tend to think we have to find it in some usual way. But that doesn't happen very often. Most of the time, our visions manifest through means that have no apparent connection to logical avenues. Nevertheless, my students often want me to convey these logical avenues to them, rather than convey my truth.

Earlier, I mentioned that I found my graphic artist for this book while I was in the process of renting cross-country skis. I didn't find him by looking in the usual places for graphic artists.

---

[1] She is Mary Robinson and her book is titled *You Are A Success*, published 1991 by Heart Publishing & Productions.

He wasn't recommended to me, and he hadn't taken out an ad anywhere. When I tell others how I achieved this goal, they say, "YES BUT, how am I going to achieve that goal?" I tell them that I went through my day, taking care of fun and business as usual, keeping my eyes open for the kind of artistic ideas I was seeking.

While I was renting the skis, I noticed drawings and paintings all over the walls that presented the feeling I was after. I asked who the artist was and found out he was young and only slightly experienced in graphic artwork. I also learned he was trying to break into the business but had not found an avenue yet. Oh, I had sought out professional graphic artists for samples of their work. Though they were excellent, they did not convey what I was looking for. I did not find my graphic artist in the accepted way.

My students repeat, "YES BUT, how am I going to find my graphic artist?" They are obviously looking for a truth that feels more reliable to them. In my desire to help my students, I am often tempted to guide them toward what they want—the usual, more acceptable, more believable way. When I attempt to do this, I am no longer teaching, but giving advice. It is important for me to stick with my own truth. If it does not feel to them like the way to achieve their goal, they will seek another teacher whose truth is more comfortable to them. What I have learned to do is to refer them, if I can, to someone who has succeeded the way they want to succeed.

Back when students were apprentices, they studied their trades under the tradespeople themselves. A student of weaving learned from a weaver. The teachers' names were usually indicative of their trade: Jane *Blacksmith*, John *Shoemaker*, Matthew *Mason*. (Wouldn't it be great if we could still identify our teachers by their names? We would find Greta *Greatrelationshipwithspouse* and Lawrence *Loveshiscareer*.) These tradespeople knew that teaching their trade secrets to apprentices enhanced their own trade. They also shared their new techniques freely with other tradespeople. They enhanced each other. This is why teaching our own truth is such an important risk to take. We can best enhance another person through our own personal experience.

When we allow ourselves to be guided by intuition, we tend to feel as though we are riding in a car without a driver. Just the opposite is true; intuition is the driver, and it steers us through all traffic jams as if there were no obstacles at all. Fully comprehending this fact is often difficult—until it is tested.

Teach your truth, and the universe will respond. The rose eventually drops its seeds. Its petals fall to the ground to be used as compost for other plants to grow within; its own plant included. Does it die? It appears to. But the rose is merely a product of the plant on which it grows. When its seeds have been spread (when the teaching is done), that rose has completed its cycle of manifestation (your vision has come full circle). The plant gets to rest for the winter. And so do you.

RESPONSE #6

Recess

	Risk		Universal Response
#1	Believing	→	Vision
#2	Choosing	→	Direction
#3	Action	→	Details
#4	Integrity	→	Miracles
#5	Acknowledgment	→	Students
#6	**Teaching**	**LEADS TO**	**Recess**

*O*nce you've done some teaching, you will have the realization that what once appeared to be risky was never a risk at all. You'll still be believing, choosing, taking action, practicing integrity, acknowledging and teaching; it's just that they will no longer feel risky where this particular vision of yours is concerned. This is the beginning of a recess; a rest from the intensity of taking risks.

The first part of this resting period is very pleasant. We are enjoying the fruits of our labors. We may have become more popular in certain circles because of our achievements. We receive more friendly phone calls, more social invitations, and our lists of friends and acquaintances are growing. We are living and experiencing our dreams, and it's downright fun.

Resting is also a period of letting go. You will observe your "students" as they continue to struggle with their beliefs, their choices, their actions, their integrity, their acknowledgments and their own teaching. You will remember how it felt, and you will often want to reach out and shake the faith into them. Then you let go and know they will find their way eventually, because you found your way.

As the rest period moves on, the novelty of this particular dream begins to wear off. The joy we experienced as the result of manifesting our dream dissipates with familiarity.

It's very much like landing a new job. First, there's the risky feeling of the interview, then the anxiety of waiting and wondering, then the excitement at having been selected, then the serenity at having a secure income. Then ... familiarity sets in. Forgotten is the excitement at having landed the job. Our gratitude for the regular paycheck becomes entangled in the daily grind of our tasks. Soon we begin to want something more than just the job.

Boredom and Lulls

At this time, we may feel as if our lives are in a rut. Nothing seems to be growing or changing. Serenity is a nice feeling ... for a while. Then we get restless.

A man I know has finally found an avenue for financial abundance. He has an unlimited amount of income and never has a worry about his bills. He can eat extravagantly, travel wherever he chooses, live in a beautiful environment and buy the best clothing. Now he is experiencing frustration and boredom. He doesn't know what he wants to do with his life.

Most of us think that having money makes all things possible, but this is only true if we know what we want. This man is at a resting point, a lull; and he is beginning to worry about himself. He thinks there is something wrong with his life.

All of us have been at this stage. Somehow we have accepted the idea that our lives should never pause. We are supposed to be striving for something all the time.

Some of the greatest musical composers were people who would write their music non-stop for three or four months. They would barely sleep or eat during this time. When the project was finished, they would have no creative musical ideas for months at a time. This was the resting period. Many of those composers suffered depression through this period, while others accepted it as natural and enjoyed it.

We make the choice to either feel guilty over this resting period or to feel serene and refreshed. When we have done the teaching, we rest. Even God rested after teaching Adam and Eve.

Is that all there is ...?

There was a song a few years ago that had a refrain that went, "Is that all there is? Is that all there is? If that's all there is, my friend, then let's keep dancing ..." The temptation during this recess period is to see ourselves as worthless. Perspective gets a little warped. Even though we have accomplished much and helped others on the road of accomplishment, we find ourselves asking the question, "Is that all there is?"

The excitement of risk-taking appears to be over. When what once appeared to be risky is no longer feeling risky, our hearts slow down, our minds are not filled with "what ifs," and we enter a stage of nothingness. The feeling of serenity begins to turn into a feeling of boredom.

We have forgotten that the feeling of excitement we had enjoyed was the result of walking into unfamiliar territory. With the anticipation of our desires spurring us along, our minds and hearts were stimulated. Now that those desires have manifested and we see how easy they were to accomplish, we wonder what all the frenzy was about. And we wonder if we'll ever feel the excitement of that frenzy again.

The challenge of the chase has ended. We succeeded in our endeavors. We got what we wanted. We have been dreaming of this end result for eons, and now it is reality; there is no dream anymore.

We have all experienced this sense of hanging in limbo, some to a greater degree than others. It all depends upon the amount of time and energy we have expended awaiting the achievement of a particular dream. The longer we have been focused upon one vision, the more humdrum our lives appear to be once we have achieved it.

The vision had become a part of our individual identities. Once it became reality, and others learned from our successes, we became different people than we were. Our identities have changed, and any kind of change means readjustment.

Changing Focus

I used to be Casey Chaney, a public school music teacher who had dreamed of working for herself in her own home for 15 years. Once that was accomplished, who was I? I looked basically the same, only my identity had changed. Now I write books and give workshops on the books I write. I speak in front of large adult audiences. This is very different from my former identity. I call myself an author today, not a public school music teacher. That was a difficult transition in itself. People would ask me what I did for a living, and I would stumble over the words.

This resting period is the time to refocus. It is an absolutely essential part of re-evaluating our new identities. We realize that we are different than we were. The old vision has manifested, and it is now time for new vision. As I said before, it may be more difficult to change focus if our focus has been the same for a long time. We have had no practice focusing on anything else.

This is one of the reasons why the wealthy man I mentioned earlier has difficulty knowing what to do with his life. His focus for many years was to achieve a regular flow of prosperity. He accomplished that. Now what? Most of us think that if only we had that kind of money we would know precisely what to do with it. We don't realize that that particular focus is an end result in itself. Once there, all of the other dreams come true, too. The car we want, the vacation we want, the education we want for our kids, the help we want to give others; these are all accomplished once we become prosperous. There appears to be no more long-term dream to desire, nurture and enjoy.

Even when we accomplish one part of a dream, we find this rest period to be a source of discouragement. Am I ever going to see carpeting in this new added room to our house? Now that I have moved where I thought I wanted to be, will I ever find the job I want? Now that the kids are all out of the house and we have our privacy, what do we do with it?

We are challenged, during this time of rest, to dream on. The lull can be deceiving. We find ourselves humming the strains of "Is that all there is …?" Walking through our fears successfully has given us a new perspective. We are different in attitude, different in thought. We are able to believe in a much bigger way because we now have the personal experience to fuel that belief. But if we don't exercise our new attitudes, we may fall back into our old fears, forgetting that all things are possible.

The way we keep believing in possibility is through contemplation and meditation. The universe has provided this rest period as the perfect opportunity in which to practice the art of contemplation and meditation. As we accept the challenge to risk again, the Power of the Ultimate Partnership begins the process of moving us forward again. What!? Another risk? You bet.

RISK #7

The Risk To
Contemplate & Meditate

	Risk		Universal Response
#1	Believing	→	Vision
#2	Choosing	→	Direction
#3	Action	→	Details
#4	Integrity	→	Miracles
#5	Acknowledgment	→	Students
#6	Teaching	→	Recess
#7	**Contemplating & Meditating**		

Contemplation and meditation are the risks we take in order to dream bigger dreams. They are risks because: a) they appear to be "do-nothing" things to do and they don't feel like they are going to help us to achieve anything; b) when we have contemplated in the past, we have been accused of daydreaming and not paying attention; and c) exposure to meditation has been through the observation of "odd" people (those from other countries, or "hippies," or people who don't dress or act according to the masses). We mày think to ourselves, "How is sitting around going to help me to achieve my dreams?" or "People will think I'm really weird."

The truth is that most successful people take time to sit quietly and contemplate positive thoughts. They follow this contemplation time with meditation so that their positive thoughts can sink in and digest.

Contemplation

Contemplation is possibility thinking. We contemplate the possible meanings of words, the possible nature of God, the possible aspects of seemingly impossible situations. It is the passageway to greater believing. Just by our willingness to contemplate we are telling the universe that we believe in greater possibilities. Contemplation is the process of opening up the floodgates of our minds and letting endless ideas pour forth.

When I am unable to come up with the right words to explain a concept, I take a walk. This is the time I allow the universe to fill or empty my mind (depending upon which is needed). When I wrote the chapter on teaching, I was having a difficult time coming up with an analogy. I took a walk around my neighborhood and contemplated how the roses were blooming and dropping their seeds. This gave me the analogy I was seeking.

There are no rules for contemplation. When I am depressed or have difficulty perceiving any direction for my life at a given moment, I pull out a spiritual book and read a paragraph or two.

The topic almost always applies to at least one thing I am concerned about. As I think about the possibilities embedded in the words, I am contemplating.

As I lie on the grass in my back yard and gaze at the clouds, enjoying their creative shapes, I am contemplating. As I listen to a speaker and find myself relaxed and daydreaming, I am contemplating. As I write my books, thinking about the message I'm attempting to convey, I am contemplating. As I seek understanding or guidance on a particular issue, I am contemplating. As I am taking a personal inventory of myself and my life, I am contemplating.

We all contemplate regularly. It happens to us naturally throughout our day, though we usually are not aware of it. Now we are awakening to the fact that we can consciously guide our contemplation. We become awake to the fact that we can think on a specific idea. We choose that idea in order to clarify or strengthen our understanding of it.

Here's one example of how I contemplate consciously:

I begin by deciding on my focus. Let's say I want to explore the idea of success. I start with a question, then I answer myself.

Question: *How do I succeed?* Answer: *I believe, I choose, I act, I practice unconditional integrity, I acknowledge, I teach, and I take time to contemplate and meditate. That's it. Everything else seems to fall right into place. It doesn't always appear to be falling right into place, but it is. My job is to risk and let the universe respond.*

Sometimes I write out certain ideas and then think on them. Using the example above, I might choose the word *how*. I ask myself questions like, "What does *how* mean?" Other times I would choose an entire phrase—*It doesn't always appear to be falling right into place, but it is.* Then I might combine the two— *It doesn't always appear to be falling right into place, but it is. How is it falling into place?* I am not trying to come up with any answers; I just allow myself to think, to contemplate. If an answer comes as the result of my contemplation, that's great. But it doesn't have to.

I don't always feel like contemplating. I make the time for it, but that doesn't always mean I end up contemplating. My contemplation might begin while I'm doing the dishes or changing the oil of the car. I may start contemplating one idea and end up in the opposite direction. Contemplation is simply exercising and expanding the capacity for believing. When we contemplate, we realize that there are greater visions.

I think over my past achievements and how they all began. I remember believing and experiencing the joy of vision; choosing and experiencing a strong sense of direction; taking action and watching the details come together; practicing integrity and realizing miracles; acknowledging the miracles and noticing that people want to learn from me; teaching and feeling the satisfaction at having accomplished something. As I think on all of these things, new thoughts automatically enter my mind. These new thoughts, filled with possibilities, become the impetus for greater dreams.

Meditation

Meditation is the art of quieting the mind so that it can absorb what has just been contemplated. If you think of contemplation as the act of turning on a water faucet, meditation is the sponge that absorbs that water. A busy mind is like a sponge that keeps squeezing its water in and out. A quiet mind is the sponge that just lies there and allows the water to be absorbed.

Accomplishing a successful meditation is not as overwhelming as it may appear. We often have an image of a meditator who sits for hours on end in a perfect state of peace. This is not the average meditator. All meditation, whether short or long in duration, is beneficial.

The goal of meditation is to rest our thoughts long enough to absorb the truth in what we have contemplated. While contemplating positive images, our skepticism and disbelieving thoughts tend to butt in. Meditation silences those thoughts so that truth can penetrate.

Truth is freedom. It feels good. Thoughts that are negative and painful in nature are not truth, even though they seem real enough. They will dissipate naturally when we meditate. Truth is real and has substance. This substance becomes understanding when we meditate, which helps us to believe in the unlimited nature of the possibilities we have contemplated.

How Should I Meditate?

There are as many different ways to meditate as there are different people in the world. For the most part, anything you can do to rest your thoughts for a while is meditation.

To begin meditation, set aside about ten minutes where you will be left alone without interruption. If you have children, use the time when they are sleeping or when they are at school. Find a position in which you are sitting upright and are comfortable.[2]

---

[2] Some people enjoy meditating lying down. This can be effective unless you fall asleep. Sleep does not quiet the mind. Dreams, which take place while we are in a state of sleep, are thoughts. If you are a person who has difficulty falling asleep, meditating while lying down may help you. But if you want to attain the benefits of meditation, you will want to stay awake.

If you are uncomfortable, you will start thinking about your discomfort. Since your goal is to rest your thoughts, being uncomfortable makes that increasingly difficult. Fold your legs if it's comfortable, stretch them out if it's not. Don't try to live up to some image you have seen. More people have ceased meditating because they couldn't be comfortable meditating the way they have seen others meditate. Be yourself. Use whatever position is best for you.

As we meditate, we strive to focus on something very simple in order to avoid focusing on everything else. That's about the closest a beginning meditator can get to quieting his/her thoughts. Also, we don't think about what we are focusing upon; we just notice it.

The reason some people touch their thumb and index finger together as they meditate is to achieve a point of focus. They concentrate on the point where their fingers touch each other and keep their thought on that point.

Others will use their natural breathing to focus upon. If you notice the edge of your nostrils where the air goes in and out, you will have a point of focus. For those of you who do not breathe well through your nose, you can notice your diaphragm going in and out as you inhale and exhale.

You can meditate with your eyes open, focusing upon the flame of a candle or any other single point. You can close your eyes and "see" a piece of fruit. Whatever your focus, as long as you are only noticing it and not thinking about it, you are meditating.

When I first flew on the little airplane that looked more like a mosquito, I had so many stomach butterflies from my fear that I thought I was going to jump out of my skin. I began to meditate by taking a deep, comfortable breath and closing my eyes. My focus, for some reason unbeknownst to me, is my dog's tennis ball. It just popped into my head one day when I was first learning to meditate. Anyway, as I brought the tennis ball into focus, my butterflies disappeared immediately. This is because my fear was due to my fearful thoughts. As I "shut off" my other thoughts in order to focus on the tennis ball, I shut off the fear as well. When I would become unfocused from the tennis ball, the butterflies were back. It was so dramatic a change, each time I would vacillate between focused and unfocused, that I began to play with my meditation. I would become unfocused purposely to see what would happen. Then I would become focused again and notice how the butterflies would be gone. Before I realized it, the plane was landing and I was perfectly fine.

Am I Doing This Right?

As you meditate, expect these things to happen:

1) Expect to lose your concentration over and over again. This is natural. It is the process of letting go of whatever thoughts bubble up while you are focusing. Gently bring back your focus as soon as you are aware that it is gone. Think of this as a mental exercise.

2) Expect to be interrupted. You might itch or feel discomfort in your muscles. You might hear the sounds around you or notice a particular odor. Each time something distracts you, name it according to the essence of what it is and then return to your focus.

For example, let's say a dog is barking. I will say to myself, "Hearing, hearing," and then I will refocus. I don't want to be specific about the sound itself, otherwise I begin thinking about the dog, its size, color, etc. If I am distracted by an itch, I say to myself, "Feeling, feeling," (as opposed to "Itching,

itching") and then I refocus. If I am distracted by my own thoughts, I say to myself, "Thinking, thinking," (as opposed to "The bills, the bills") and then I refocus.

3) Expect to try different ways of meditating. If you are just beginning to meditate, you will feel awkward. It's no different than learning to ride a bike for the first time. Simply adjust yourself and get back on. You may change your method several times before getting comfortable with any one in particular, and even then, you may vary positions, focal points and times allotted.

4) Expect to feel as if nothing in you has changed after meditating. Change is gradual. Eventually, you will notice your level of belief increasing, and you may even find yourself using your meditation techniques in your daily experiences. I learned to practice the art of focusing when I would have an argument with my spouse. I would catch myself not listening to what she was saying as I was trying to interrupt her with my comeback. At that time I would bring myself back into focus upon her words instead of my angry thoughts. It has enhanced my ability to be a good listener and to detach in a healthy way from her anger. This way, I can really hear the true message that is being camouflaged by any negativity.

5) Expect to find meditating exhausting at first. As I mentioned before, doing anything new takes adjustment, and adjustment is sometimes tiresome. As you do a little meditating every day, even for short periods at a time, it will become increasingly easy and relaxing.

6) Expect to possibly lose interest in meditating after a few times. If this happens, you can always come back to it another time. Also, you may be doing your own form of meditation without even knowing it.

Whatever happens, consider it perfectly appropriate. This is your process of personal growth and development, and no one else can tell you whether you are doing it the right way.

If you really want to delve extensively into meditation, there is an abundant variety of sources for learning about it. Your public library will have a section specifically on meditation, and almost all general bookstores will carry books on meditation techniques. You can take classes and workshops on meditation from colleges, churches, health clubs and many other social organizations. Make it fun.

The Benefits Of Contemplation & Meditation

The main benefit of contemplation and meditation is stability. Contemplating and meditating enhances your depth of belief. As unlimited ideas and truth settle into your consciousness, you will be more sure of yourself and your abilities to achieve. Your dreams, desires and ideas will become even clearer to you than they have been, and your vision will get bigger.

Life is actually a series of visions that move into greater visions. We simply glide from one to the next. As is true with all of the other six risks and responses, this process of the Ultimate Partnership happens naturally. When we become awakened to the process, we can see where we may be stuck and take whatever risks are necessary to start the ball rolling again.

Contemplation and meditation is the push that moves us from one dream, desire or idea to the next. At the point where we feel stagnant in our lives, contemplation and meditation is a call for the universe to respond again.

RESPONSE #7

Greater Vision

	Risk		Universal Response
#1	Believing	→	Vision
#2	Choosing	→	Direction
#3	Action	→	Details
#4	Integrity	→	Miracles
#5	Acknowledgment	→	Students
#6	Teaching	→	Recess
#7	Contemplating & Meditating	LEADS TO	Greater Visions

*C*ontemplation and meditation bring about a greater vision. As we contemplate possibility and quiet our opposing thoughts, we become privy to a greater vision than the one most recently achieved.

There is really no beginning dream, though it often appears as if there is. If we think about the thoughts and achievements that came before a particular dream was conceived, we will see how each one led to the next. I want to illustrate this concept, and for the sake of clarity, I will start this discussion at the point of my first book, a dream that came as the result of many others.

I decided to write a book. The vision was the finished book, cover and all. The day the finished product arrived from the printer I sat down and took time to contemplate and meditate. The new vision was of the book being sold in the bookstores. Once that happened, the excitement and exhilaration were over; there was a lull. What now? Contemplation and meditation; new dreams. Workshops, seminars, classes, traveling and speaking. I've now come quite a ways from just seeing the book in print. More contemplation and meditation; greater dreams.

All throughout this process of developing new dreams, I am taking risks and experiencing the responses from the universe. I may have a new dream, but do I really believe it will be possible? The cycle of the Ultimate Partnership begins again:

1) I risk believing that this new dream will be possible, and my vision becomes clearer. I see my choices.

2) I risk choosing, specifying and prioritizing. I feel directed through the experience of the 4 I's—Inspiration, Imagination, Intuition and Incitement.

3) I risk taking direct action on my 4 I's. I watch as the details of timing, people, places, situations and money begin to move as the result of my move.

4) I risk practicing integrity—honesty, generosity and good-will—even when I don't want to, or when I am afraid to. I marvel at the miraculous results that begin to manifest.

5) I risk acknowledging the miracles, and I find myself surrounded by "students."

6) I risk teaching, and I discover the feeling of accomplishment followed by the desire for more.

7) I risk contemplating and meditating, and I feel the stability of my new identity, followed by greater visions.

There's a wonderful biblical story about a woman named Sarah and her husband, Abraham. In their ripe old age Sarah and Abraham are told that they will conceive and give birth to the child they had always wanted. Their first response to this information was to laugh. At 90 years old, this seemed ludicrous. Abraham is directed by God to look toward the heavens and "count the stars, if you are able to count them." Abraham understands the message—there are endless possibilities. One year later they gave birth to a son, Isaac.

What are your greater visions? Look at the stars on a clear night and remember that there are stars even beyond those. There is no end to what we can all accomplish if only we are willing to take the risks. Risk-taking is risk-*free*. There is incredible joy to experience through risk. Look for the possibility in everything, and you will never feel limited by your fears again.

Profiles In Courage

My belief in the Ultimate Partnership has enabled me to take risks that I would not have otherwise taken. The universe, responding to my direct action, brought all of the right pieces together to manifest my vision. The Power of the Ultimate Partnership was greater than any of the tasks I was facing.

When I talk with people who are dissatisfied with certain aspects of their lives, I notice a common bond between them. They are unwilling to take big risks in order to alter their unhappy situations. They seem to think that risk-taking is easier or more convenient for other people. They are quick to point out how other people are better prepared to take risks. They believe that risk-takers have either tied up all of their loose ends or that risk-takers somehow have more personal, emotional or financial support. This belief is quite erroneous.

The following stories were related to me by people who consider themselves risk-takers. The one common bond between them is that they all feel fear when they step into unfamiliar territory. It seems that almost everyone who risks, does so uncomfortably; but the determination to be happy overcomes the fear. Other than that, there is no other common bond. They are as diverse as the non-risk-takers.

In other words, the only difference between non-risk-takers

and risk-takers is that the risk-takers are possibility thinkers. They believe.

The Risk To Believe—Pat

"Pat" is a woman who risked believing in possibility. She related her story to me many years ago in an effort to help me understand the concept of "letting go." As the direct result of her "teaching," I began to risk. It is to "Pat," whose real name I can't remember, that I dedicate this section of Ready, Willing and Terrified.

Before Pat and her husband were married, they agreed that he would work and pay the bills, and that she would cook, clean and raise the kids. This is the way they both wanted it, and Pat believed that she was about to live her dream.

Shortly after they were married, Pat learned that her husband was an active alcoholic. Along with that came the realization that he was not going to live up to his end of the pre-nuptial agreement. He was not paying the bills, nor was there even enough money with which to pay them. He was working, but most of the money was going toward alcohol.

By the time three children had arrived, Pat was cooking, cleaning, raising the kids with no help from her husband, working part-time and paying all of the bills. This was most definitely not her dream.

The thought of leaving her marriage had entered Pat's mind numerous times. But due to her deep religious beliefs, she was convinced that marriages were to be worked out, beyond the problems. She believed in the possibility that her life could get better without leaving her marriage.

Pat sought help and was introduced to the Al-anon program. Al-anon is a 12-step organization dedicated to helping individuals who have friends or family members addicted to alcohol. During this time, her husband continued drinking, and she continued working and paying the bills.

Pat began attending Al-anon meetings regularly. She listened to the success stories of others and wondered how she could apply their ideas to her own life. One day, another member asked her if she really believed that God would take care of her, no matter what. Pat's answer was a definite "yes ... sort of."

This set Pat to thinking. If she really believed that God would take care of her, no matter what, then why was she doing all of the things she did not want to do? After much fear, apprehension and anxiety, she decided to put her belief into action. She decided to stop working part-time, and she decided to no longer pay the bills. She would live up to her end of the agreement by cooking, cleaning and taking care of the kids.

This decision threatened every part of Pat's existence. What if there was not enough money to buy food for her children? What if the utilities were turned off? How could she care for her family properly? What kind of a mother was she, anyway? What kind of a mother would allow her children to go without heat or food or clothing? What kind of a mother would stay in an alcoholic home? She was terrified that her children would be taken away from her. She was also frightened of her husband's response. He had a violent streak about him when he drank, and she feared for her safety.

In addition to her fears, her ego would have to take a beating. What would the neighbors think? Up until now, she had been able to put up the front of having the perfect family. What if she had to reach out to them for help? That would mean admitting to them that her family had problems—serious problems. She was not accustomed to airing out her dirty laundry with strangers.

Through all of the fears and "what ifs," Pat kept coming back to her belief. She had begun to feel like a hypocrite. She professed a strong belief in the power of God, and yet she refused to trust that this power would somehow care for her. She realized that nothing was changing by repeating the same sequence of events, day in and day out.

Finally, Pat took the risk to believe 100 percent. She quit her part-time job and left the bills unopened on the desk for her husband to see. Rather than get into a useless confrontation with her soused spouse, Pat just went about her business doing what she had always wanted to do. She cooked, cleaned the house and became actively involved with her children. The other Al-anon members were a great support group during this time. They did not tell her what to do or how to do it. They just encouraged her and were there with inspiration when she would become panicked over the consequences of her risky decisions.

Two months went by without incident. There was enough money for food, but then the bills weren't being paid. One day, the gas stopped working. She couldn't cook on her stove, and there was no hot water. She fired up the barbecue and acted as if they were camping. She had already humbled herself with her neighbors by explaining to them what she was attempting to do and asked them for assistance. They respected her courage and, without hesitation, offered her the use of their homes.

In the meantime, her husband suddenly found his showers frighteningly cold. He asked her what was wrong and she suggested he call the gas company. She made it clear that she was not going to do the calling. When he found out the bills had not been paid, he angrily asked her about it. She reminded him of their agreement and said, "That's not my job." He wasn't happy with her decision, and he ranted and raved all evening. She stayed out of his way and let him rave.

The following day, the electricity was shut off. Pat brought out the candles. By this time, she had become very good friends with the neighbors, whom she had avoided during the previous five years. Together, they were enjoying the humor of the situation.

Two days after the electricity was shut off, Pat awakened to a warm house. The lights came on and she could cook on her stove again. Her husband had begun paying the bills. The lights went off one more time a couple of months later, but they have stayed on ever since.

She learned how to ignore his drinking and treat him with love, regardless of the way he was. They quit having terrible arguments because she refused to argue with him when he was drunk. She began to acknowledge the good times they had together when he was sober, rather than focusing on the bad times when he was drinking. They now had a social life with their neighbors and others from organizations Pat had become involved with through her children.

Three years had passed by the time Pat related her story to me. Her husband was still drinking, but she was enjoying her life. She made it a point to do whatever she wanted to do, while still being a responsible spouse and mother. The result for her was a successful marriage regardless of the alcoholism. Her courage was enhanced by her decision to believe, and she was able to risk in other areas of her life as well.

The last thing she said to me was this: "If you really believe, your decisions and actions will bear witness to that belief." It changed my life.

The Risk To Choose—Linda

Linda was in private practice as a counselor specializing in eating disorders and other addictions treatment. Her practice had increased substantially over the years, and her reputation was growing rapidly through her speaking and workshops.

Regardless of her success, Linda was becoming restless, and she was feeling confined. She wanted to move on to something different. With only a vague sense of what she would do afterward, she left her practice.

For the next year Linda attempted to follow her inspiration, imagination, intuition and incitement. This led her toward a variety of new people and experiences. At first, she started a marketing business that drained her energy as well as her resources. Her 4 I's told her to let go of that business, and she initially struggled with feelings of failure. Upon further reflection, she realized that, due to her experience with that business, she acquired some great leadership and people skills. She became acutely aware of her personal strengths and weaknesses, which served to guide her into new endeavors.

Over the past year, Linda has grown in her belief in the Power of God as her Ultimate Partnership. However, she was not prepared for her husband's decision to quit his high-tech management position. Exactly one year after she left her practice, he left his job. Although it was a mutual decision based on several factors—his health and his unhappiness with the company—it was difficult for Linda to accept the reality of both of them being without jobs.

She experienced the feelings of anger, fear and excitement—fear being the primary of these. There is a significant difference between intellectual awareness of the Partnership and actually testing it out. Linda says she vacillates between seeing the proof of it and discounting the proof. Her "what ifs" close in on her every now and then, and she has to take time to clean up her perception of the situation.

Having no job has its advantages, though. Choice making is wide open. The trick is to follow your heart—your vision—and that is what Linda began to do. She happened to be taking a walk with a friend one day and decided to stop into a mall that she normally would have avoided. Its stores sold non-essential items, frilly things that Linda had little interest in. In the back was one store that caught her eye. It was filled with non-essentials, as she expected, but there was one item that attracted her. It was a magic wand, complete with lace and ribbons, silk and delicate butter-flies.

Linda had been developing some women's groups that, as a part of the activity, included some simple rituals. She thought the magic wand would fit right in. Even though her pessimistic "what ifs" started nagging at her, she arranged to buy the wands wholesale and sell them to her clients or anyone else who might want one.

Meanwhile, her mind was also focused on her wedding ring. Linda's mother-in-law had given Linda a ring to use as a wedding ring. Though it was very beautiful, Linda never quite felt like it was hers. She knew which ring she really wanted and, even though there was very little money available for the bills, let alone a ring, the ring seemed more important. It was a priority in her heart. After talking with her husband about it, they agreed to make a down payment on the ring. Practically speaking, this made no sense whatsoever. But Linda had become accustomed to following her inner guide, and for some reason, getting the ring felt like the thing to do.

After making her first payment on the ring, Linda went to her office, which was a small room that she had rented inexpensively in a local church. She brought the magic wand to show to the wedding coordinator of the church, and the woman loved it. The coordinator ran down the halls with it showing everyone she knew, and when she returned she had an order for ten wands! That order put Linda into business, and the bills and the ring were paid.

Sometimes the choices don't appear to be logical. Linda has learned through faith and, ultimately experience, that making those choices opens up possibilities never before considered.

The Risk To Take Action—Greg

Greg was attending school and was very committed to completing his program of study. He still owed money for the previous semester and had no idea how he was going to create the funds to attend spring term. The school made it clear that all past debts must be paid before registration could be accepted for the following term. In addition, they could offer no more than half of the full tuition in financial assistance. This would not have been enough to make it possible for Greg to attend.

During this time, Greg had taken my class on risk-taking. He had come to believe in the Ultimate Partnership, and he knew in his heart that taking risks would provide the necessary response from the universe. So, with firm conviction, he was determined to put his belief into action.

By purchasing the books for his classes, he was acting as if his education was a sure thing. He then told all of his classmates that he would indeed be in class with them in the spring. When the time came to actually register for the classes, Greg still did not have the money. Regardless of the pessimistic outlook, he filled out his registration form and sent it in, along with an explanation of his needs.

One week later, an administrator from the school called Greg and offered him an alternative. In exchange for part-time maintenance work around the school, Greg would receive free tuition and a waiver of all of his past debts. The work Greg was to take on was directly related to his course of study.

Believing in possibility opened up Greg's mind to visualize a miracle. The inspiration, imagination, intuition and incitement came naturally as the result, and it guided him toward the action he could take. Taking that action set the universe in motion, and everything ultimately came together to manifest his vision.

The Risk To Practice Integrity—Rick

Rick was recently separated from his wife after only one year of marriage. He had been living a life of heavy drinking, some drug use and a rather cynical attitude toward people in general. The breakup of his marriage devastated him, and he decided that some major changes were necessary. He stopped all drinking and drug use and began attending church.

As Rick became a different person, he didn't enjoy his old friendships any longer, and they, in turn, did not appreciate his changes. He moved to a new state where he could be closer to his family. He secured a very good job and began to work toward becoming the kind of person he wanted to be.

What this meant for Rick was that he learned to love, instead of judge others. It also meant removing himself from conversations that were gossipy or crude in nature.

The environment in which he was working consisted of a group of people who engaged in the kind of talk and behaviors that Rick was attempting to avoid. He found it difficult not to judge them, but he found it even more difficult not to indulge in his old habits. Every time a group of them began talking, and the conversation turned crude or negative, Rick would join in. Afterward, he would be upset with himself.

He decided that he needed to put some integrity principles into practice. This was a risk for Rick. He didn't want to appear to have a "holier than thou" attitude. He liked the people he worked with; he just didn't want to do some of the things they were doing. He was afraid he would ostracize himself from everyone if he refused to participate in their conversations.

After discussing his dilemma with his family, he came up with some ideas for applying integrity to his own life without alienating his co-workers. The opportunity to test his new foundation came the very next day.

The discussion began as usual, with some derogatory gossip. Rick stood back and listened without joining the interchange. When asked for his opinion, Rick tactfully explained a bit about what he was trying to change in his life and how gossiping was harmful to him. He made it clear that he was not upset with them for their part, just that he needed to avoid practicing that kind of behavior in his own life in order to survive. Due to Rick's sincerity, his co-workers responded with understanding. They respected his honesty enough that they did not tease him about his new beliefs.

Though he had not severed his healthy working relationships with his co-workers, he longed to work in an environment with people who had more in common with himself. Soon after Rick risked practicing integrity principles, he was offered a promotion that took him to a different location. The people at the new location were on the same spiritual path as he was. At this point, Rick realized that his integrity automatically drew him toward others with whom he could share more than just shop talk.

The Risk To Acknowledge—Mariah

As I was writing this section of *Ready, Willing and Terrified*, I had asked several people to write an account of their own risk stories for me. One of these stories came from a friend of mine named Mariah. When she pulled out her story, she said rather sheepishly, "It turned out to be nine pages long."

Mariah read her story to me, and as I listened I became acutely aware of the way she acknowledged her miracles. The story was detailed and contained acknowledgment of people, places, feelings, timing and situations.

In her own words: "I think I've been risking all my life and just didn't realize it, or didn't have the self-esteem to fully take it in and honor it. People around me have always remarked about the wonderful adventures I've been in, and for quite a while my response would be this, 'huh?'

"… my greatest experiences have occurred in response to my hearing the Truth within me and following through with it. I might stammer, fret and cry when the notion comes up; that just seems to be my way of allowing and acknowledging the fear before I take the steps."

Some of the miracles Mariah acknowledged are usually not considered miracles. She was diagnosed as diabetic, she was miserable at her job, she was financially broke, she lost a lover. Mariah considers all of these circumstances miracles because overcoming them meant stepping into unfamiliar territory— taking risks. In so doing, she was introduced to more miracles: organizations and people who inspired her to succeed, better food, Tai Chi (a martial art form), quitting a stressful job, self-responsibility and loving herself more. These, in turn, led her to still greater miracles: incredible circumstances that came together enabling her to attend a restful and directing retreat in Hawaii, the courage to follow her heart in finding her right place in the world, the intuition for creating healthy relationships with others.

Mariah has taken time to focus on the good within each situation, and the results are obvious. As soon as she became honest about her desires in life and believed that they were possible, her energy level for achieving those desires increased. She takes action, practices integrity and joyfully acknowledges the miracles.

Having a similar circle of friends, I hear the comments of the "students" she has "taught." They respect the choices she makes, and they look forward to spending time with her. They say things like, "If Mariah can do it, so can I." That's acknowledgment.

The Risk To Teach—Jean

Jean is a staff nurse in the emergency room of a university hospital. In 1980, she was diagnosed with ovarian cancer. She went into remission until 1988, when there was a re-occurrence.

There are many different kinds of pain, and Jean has experienced most of them throughout this ordeal. There is the pain of the fear and anxiety she felt upon hearing the diagnosis of cancer. There is the pain of coming to terms with the prognosis. There is the pain of the many invasive procedures performed on her body, such as blood being drawn, radiation, chemotherapy, etc. There is the pain of people's fear, pity and judgments; and the pain of hearing people minimize her suffering.

Jean knows exactly how others feel when they have been diagnosed with cancer. This understanding led her to co-found an organization whose purpose is to give encouragement, hope and support to women who have been diagnosed with gynecological cancers.

Though Jean's cancer is now again in remission, she continues to work with others in helping them to overcome their pain. The essence of teaching is sharing what we've learned with others who are facing similar challenges.

Jean's decision to "teach" was a difficult one. For one thing, it meant talking openly about the most vulnerable part of herself—her emotions—with people she did not know. It also meant teaching those without cancer about the needs of those with it. The most difficult part of teaching for Jean is accepting the fate of those "students" whose bodies do not respond to treatment. It is a risk to create bonding relationships over and over again with people who might not live very much longer.

There is more to Jean's teaching than her experience with the painful aspects of cancer. Her experience also includes learning to live life happily despite the cancer. She enrolled in a creative visualization class to get in touch with her unfulfilled dreams and desires. One of those dreams was to go hot air ballooning. Through visualization she began to see herself riding in a hot air balloon. Jean purchased a trip to Albuquerque, New Mexico, for the October hot air balloon races, and she is looking forward to the possibility of riding in one of them.

As Jean continues to experience life and share her experiences, she teaches many more people than just the women in her support group. She teaches us all how to love our lives despite the setbacks and to live as fully as possible while we can. In Jean's own words, "I took what was a devastatingly negative experience and made it a positive one."

The Risk To Contemplate and Meditate—Berdell

Berdell is my spouse, partner, best friend and confidant. She has so many incredible talents and capabilities that, even after eight years together, I still find myself in awe as I observe her.

Some of those talents include a sharp memory and the ability to get many things done in a small amount of time. There are times when her mind is thinking so quickly that it runs ahead of her body. Then her body does whatever her mind is thinking at the moment, even though it was in the process of doing something else.

This has resulted in some rather comical situations. One time she was in the process of putting a pitcher of Kool-Aid in the refrigerator and ended up putting it in one of the kitchen cupboards instead. Another time, when she was trying to figure out what was wrong with the car, her mind was thinking so fast that she forgot she was planning to check the fuses first. Before I had a chance to ask her about it she had removed the alternator and replaced it with a new and rather expensive one. The problem turned out to be a burned out fuse.

Berdell's mind is also very organized. She spends very little time doing nothing because she has a mental planning committee on duty 24 hours a day. Yes, even in her sleep, she is preparing the next day's agenda.

All of these talents are valuable and have proven to be tremendous assets to her life. She lives by the principles of the Ultimate Partnership, and the result is that there is always a new dream to manifest and new challenges to overcome. She has been a teacher extraordinaire. She does great with all of the first six risks. Then comes the recess; the resting period after the teaching. Here is where Berdell faces her biggest risk.

She is so accustomed to having a regular run of ideas that the recess scares her. She becomes fidgety and sees herself as lacking ambition. Shortly thereafter she begins to have moments of panic and depression, fearing that this period will never end.

To contemplate and meditate has been a risk for Berdell because, in the past she has considered these things a "waste of time." With a mind that never seems to stop figuring and planning, contemplating possibilities is like getting caught at a train crossing when you're already late for an appointment. Meditation is even worse.

Recently, Berdell decided that she was not being productive when her mind wanted to work, but the universe was saying, "Recess time!" She bought some books on meditation techniques and began setting time aside to practice contemplation and meditation.

At last the moment for practice had arrived. She found a quiet place, lay down and closed her eyes. Instead of contemplating and meditating, she fell asleep. This depressed her even more than doing nothing; but believing in the Ultimate Partnership, she knew that the awkwardness would pass and she would succeed. After a week of afternoon naps, she decided this particular method of contemplation and meditation was not for her.

Berdell discovered that, for her, practicing contemplation and meditation meant reading a book, taking a leisurely drive in the car or doing the laundry or the dishes. She has found that it slows down the hustle and bustle of her organized mind and allows her to think more clearly. It has become okay for her to schedule time out for contemplation and meditation. She is seeing the results, too. She's not as anxious about getting everything done within her time limits. The time she spends working is more productive and less frantic. And there is vision—greater vision.

Berdell now sees herself as calm and serene, yet very focused (well, most of the time, anyway). She observes herself in high service to others while still attaining her own levels of success. Today, she is able to spend quality time with Corey (our son) and me on a regular basis without feeling like she is being confined or restrained.

She has learned that contemplation and meditation are time-savers, not time-wasters; that they lead to greater visions than she could come up with by her own constant planning and figuring.

"What's next," I ask her, "now that *Ready, Willing and Terrified* is written?"

"I haven't decided yet," she replies, nonchalantly. "I'm still contemplating the possibilities."

Right on.

A Personal Note

May your understanding of the Ultimate Partnership serve to make risk-taking easier. I look forward to hearing about your risks and your miracles. Here's to a more fulfilling life for us all!

NOTES